What others are saying about *Finding Church*

There is no slow bleed; the mass exodus from local congregations is a stubborn fact. So why is Wayne Jacobsen so hopeful? Because dispersion and isolation need not be the endgame. Jacobsen is *finding church*—the fully functioning family of Christ that transcends institutions—networking everywhere. I would especially invite Jesus-loving ex-churchgoers to borrow his eyes so they might share his hope.

BRAD JERSAK, Ph.D., author of *Can You Hear Me?*
Abbotsford, BC

Finding Church is a riveting and challenging read that prompts its readers to seriously reconsider the definition of church. With courage and compassion, Jacobsen states what millions of Christians intuitively know but can't admit, while sharing his passion for a church that every believer craves.

DEREK WILDER, author of *Freedom*
Life Transforming Group, Andersonville, IN

For that endless stream of people I meet who love God but either cannot bring themselves to re-enter the institutional church world or who are feeling great pain from abuses they cannot understand at the hands of leaders who subverted what we call church, Wayne Jacobsen's book will be a great encouragement. Without overlaying a new structure, he reminds us that living for and with God is far simpler than we ever imagined and that God still knows our address. Rare is the invitation to relax in God's love and love others, and it is enough.

GAYLE ERWIN, author of *The Jesus Style*
Cathedral City, CA

Finding Church is written by one who is not throwing stones. Just the opposite. His love for the church can be found on every page, even as he beckons us toward something more—the very real New Creation.

BOB PRATER, former pastor, entrepreneur
Bakersfield, CA

If you have tried every Christian conference, attended every kind of church, and gone through numerous programs for deeper spirituality, but cannot shake the "Is this all there is?" feeling, do yourself a favor and read *Finding Church*. In a gracious and loving way, Wayne Jacobsen provides encouragement, hope, and direction to all who have known that there must be something more to this thing we call church but have almost despaired of finding it. You may find that the church you long for might be sitting right next to you as you read these very words.

JEREMY MYERS, author of *Put Service Back into the Church Service,*
Portland, OR

Like all of Wayne Jacobsen's books, *Finding Church* is an engaging and graceful work that is rich in insight. He presents a simple, beautiful, and incredibly freeing picture of what it means for believers to come together, and how the community of believers can operate without an institution pulling the strings.

MICK MOONEY, author of *An Outsider's Guide to the Gospel*
Sydney, Australia

With the integrity and objectivity one hopes for from an author and based on decades of his experience and study, Wayne Jacobsen tackles one of today's growing questions in his new book *Finding Church*: Is the church a place we go or who we are? Jacobsen offers perspective and insight on ecclesiology—the nature of what is generally known as "the church." If you are ready to ask the who-what-when-where-why-and-how questions about the church then you are ready for *Finding Church*.

GREG ALBRECHT, author of *A Taste of Grace*
Plain Truth Ministries, Pasadena, CA

Wayne has always been a blessed source that gives us language to describe what we are all feeling. Be ready to put on a new pair of glasses that will allow you to see the church that has been hiding right in front of you all these years—a church free from human effort, alive in the Spirit and built by Jesus himself. By changing the focus of the conversation, Wayne opens the way to have a much more fruitful dialogue as we gaze at the church that Jesus is building.

BARRY STEINMAN, iconoclast, peacemaker, writer, and fellow pilgrim
Oceanside, CA

This book will challenge those wedded to the traditional image of the church, but don't let that scare you. This is what we have all felt sitting in the pew and rethinking our "default setting" about his church. Wayne reminds us of things we thought we knew but must learn again. The Church is not the bricks and boards of the building but the blood and bones of people in a growing relationship with each other with Jesus as the head.

NICK SEMBRANO, contributor to the Theophilus Group
Kingsburg, CA

Finding Church offers wisdom, hope, and godward, practical direction for those who have experienced frustration or hurt in man-centered systems. But it does more than that as Wayne shares the vision and certainty of Jesus building his church, his way. Wayne is uniquely positioned to write this book with years of experience in different Christian settings and then years beyond it in freedom and a growing love relationship with him. This has included travel around the world to connect with many who are joined by bonds far higher than loyalty to a leader, group, or organization. He points us to Him who is the Way and opens up the glorious potential of His headship in his people. I highly recommend it.

DAVID RICE, retired science teacher and brother on the journey
Co Wickow, Ireland

I loved this book! From the moment I started reading it, I found my heart coming alive with renewed hope for seeing and experiencing a true expression of New Testament "church life" in my generation. For years I've struggled with a gnawing sense that there had to be more to church than what I had encountered in religious institutions, but I really didn't know where to turn. After reading *Finding Church*, I've discovered that there are countless possibilities for experiencing kingdom life in the conversations and relationships I engage. I highly recommend Wayne's book.

S. J. HILL, Bible teacher and author of *Enjoying God* and *A Love for the Ages*
Cromwell, IN

It's about time someone wrote a book like *Finding Church*! Without condemning those who see it differently, Wayne has found a way to explain why people are disillusioned with our religious systems and how they are discovering a church beyond it that they find so enjoyable. He speaks for me too!

SILVIO VIOTTI, IT specialist
Vallorbe, Switzerland

Finding Church is a mature reflection on the extensive and unique experience Wayne Jacobsen has had over many years with individuals and groups who are exploring the reality of fellowship with the Father, His Son, and one another, free of the trammels of institution. The message is timely and will be strongly encouraging for others to press on in their own search for church as Father wants it to be.

JACK GRAY, retired surgeon
Auckland, New Zealand

If you find it difficult to be true to yourself while being part of a group based on religious conformity, read *Finding Church*. You'll discover it is possible to be uniquely you and, at the same time, be part of this beautiful family Jesus is building, who are encouraging, supporting, and caring as they learn to live in God's love. The church is alive and well. We only need eyes to see it the way he does.

KEVIN TUPPER, founder of Christian Simplicity, Inc.
Haymarket, VA

Each page of *Finding Church* will lead you on a compelling journey to discover a church beyond our manmade structures and behold it as the fruit of a new creation that thrives in freedom and love and depends on transformation from within not conformity imposed from without. Illustrated by experiences from his own life, Wayne shows how a culture of mutual honor, love, and respect opens the door to a oneness of heart and purpose that can transform the world. This inspiring and challenging book is a must read for all who hunger for something more than what we call church today.

DAVID FREDRICKSON, author of *The Church Has Left the Building*
Family Room Media, Citrus Heights, CA

This book is the capstone of Wayne Jacobsen's life-long quest to discover the nature of our Lord's church. It's presented without spin and without agenda, other than to live in his love. Each of Wayne's books has been the equivalent of a doctoral dissertation. Offering the same remarkable depth of insight and understanding, this is a personal best. It's not just a home run; this time he hit it out of the park.

BOB LANNING, missionary in India
Ripe Harvest Ministries, Bedford, TX

Yet again Wayne Jacobsen draws from his fascinating journey of following Jesus to produce a challenging book, *Finding Church*. And where he finds "church" may surprise you! Because church is literally anywhere where Jesus is with his followers. From helping us understand leadership to grappling with what it looks like for everyone's contribution to be important, *Finding Church* is actually a description of finding Jesus in our everyday life with His people.

TONY DALE, founder of Sedera Health and House2House
Austin, TX

Living in an age of conformity and pretense brought about by the constant pressure of religiosity to perform or else, Wayne's insights are a welcome call to change within the church community for freedom in the love offered by Jesus. His book encourages us to understand and accept that Father is looking for those who trust Him without having first to win His approval. Finally, a book that dares to confront the self-centeredness of what passes for Christianity....

DAVE COLEMAN, retired hospice chaplain
Visalia, CA

Wayne has taken his years living both as a leader inside the institutional church and outside its walls and crafted a book that reads like a conversation shared between fellow journeyers who have set out on a pilgrimage to find a treasured promise. He describes the church with conviction and deep affection, revealing that she is alive and growing all around us, within our culture and communities and even our own souls. Throughout *Finding Church*, the heartbeat of the Father and His relentless and incomprehensible love is prevalent. Wayne addresses the hard and confusing questions that invariably arise when one attempts to unglue oneself from religion, with both kindness and wisdom. This is an invaluable book for anyone who has experienced "frustration at the disparity between (their) hungers and (their) experience" in the institutional church, and a great encouragement to those who have already embarked on the journey into the unknown, outside of its walls.

JANNA LAFRANCE, author of *A Girl Named Grace*
Ajax, Ontario

Wayne Jacobsen is just like most people who will pick up this book—a sincere believer who genuinely wants to live the Christian life to the full, but who is, at the same time, very conscious of his own weaknesses, and those of the Christian church. As he tells about his personal journey, however, he reveals how, bit-by-bit, his attitude of the Christian Life and the Christian Church changed—in many positive ways. I myself found that every chapter contained insights that were hugely helpful, and I couldn't keep my highlighter away. I am convinced that any enthusiastic Christian who follows the book through will find a new zest for following Jesus and his people.

STAN FIRTH, author of The Remarkable Replacement Army
Surrey, England

Finding Church is for the weary, the restless, or the earnest disciple who longs for intimacy with Jesus and his people. It is a vision of what church could look like if we weren't spending so much time and energy attending to our institutions and instead were living in the same reality Jesus did, with an eye on his Father and compassion for people around us. Let Wayne help you discover the church Jesus is building. There really is something more.

DAN MAYHEW, author of The Butterfly and the Stone
Portland, OR

At the beginning of my detox process from organized religion I read *So You Don't Want to Go to Church Anymore*. It affirmed the feelings I had for years were not rebellion, but the prompting of the spirit to lead me away from lifeless religion. Now *Finding Church* affirms everything The Lord has been showing me over the past five years: that Jesus is the builder of the church and that we would do well to stop trying to help him. When we trust Jesus to assemble us, not merely for meetings, but organically and relationally, we experience the reality of his church and so does the world around us.

VINCE COAKLEY, radio talk show host
Charlotte, NC

In *Finding Church,* my friend Wayne Jacobsen offers Christ's way to a home for those who have searched for it congregation to congregation all their lives. The answers he offers come long after he has learned to live it and they are as free and freeing as the Gospel itself!

JOHN LYNCH, co-author of Bo's Café and The Cure
Scottsdale, AZ

Finding Church

What if there really is something more?

WAYNE JACOBSEN

Trailview Media
Newbury Park, CA

Finding Church by Wayne Jacobsen
www.findingchurch.com

International Standard Book Number
978-0-9839491-5-2

Trailview Media, an imprint of Lifestream
www.lifestream.org
1560 Newbury Road, Ste 1 #313
Newbury Park, CA 91320
(805) 498-7774
fax: (805) 499-5975
office@lifestream.org

Cover design: Dave Aldrich, www.aldrichdesign.com
Cover interiors: Nan Bishop, www.nbishopsdesigns.com

Printed in the United States of America
Original Printing

To Julie, Andrew, and Tyler
My three children, two by birth and one by marriage,
who bring great joy into my life every day.

Contents

Foreword

Wayne Jacobsen asks a compelling question in the title of his latest book, and he continues to ask the reader to consider the questions so many Christ-followers have long pondered, posed, or simply been too afraid to ask. If the resonance and comfort found in this query were the sole reasons to read this book, it would be enough. The deep sense of identification one gains from joining Wayne on this journey is a salve to the heart, cheering the long-held dream of finding a church that is so much more than a steepled edifice on the corner.

In fact, there is much more to love about this book, and I found myself engaged immediately as Wayne brings clarity to the growing trend of disengagement from the traditional church—the departure of the nones—as it has come to be known. But rather than lambast those leaving or criticize those in leadership for not addressing this exodus with compassion, he helps readers understand the many pitfalls and trappings of contemporary Christianity, pointing more toward the ecology of church structure rather than the frailties of the human heart.

Early on, Wayne puts his finger in the center of an ache that cries out from the depths of every believer who has experienced an inkling of "something more," but who has gone away empty. Yet, it is not with vinegar that he touches it. The very salve of God's love is the much-needed ointment he uses to nurture healing in the deepest parts of the heart. Thus, the reader is led to the key of the entire book, which is the knowledge that Christ-followers have the opportunity to enter into a whole new creation. Sadly, this life-changing truth is often missed by many of us for far too long and missed altogether by some. Instead we get hung up with other questions of hierarchy, gifting, and finding our own little molehill on the mountain of the Lord. When this happens, the church becomes its own personal proving ground. It is in this dastardly place that we see the simplicity of life together replaced with the all-too familiar scenario of human striving, ambition, and organizational strategies. It's here, when the Body of

Christ becomes all about personal achievement, approval, and self-actualization, that so many lose heart. The good news is, when we finally learn that our place in the family of God is simply "in Christ," we begin a new journey—one that makes the Lord Jesus central so we can look to him for leadership, guidance, comfort, and love.

These ideas are unpacked in Wayne's own inimitable way as he poses this question: "What would the church look like if it were made up of people who were learning to live in the same reality Jesus did?" I'm not sure there's a more important question to be asked. Learning to live in the reality of the risen Savior evokes a much different response to being a Christian than when asking, "What church should I attend?" What this means and how we do it together is the road that is explored throughout the rest of this helpful, invigorating book.

It is indeed the road less traveled, but one that I myself have long walked—sometimes in solitude and other times in the midst of many a fellow sojourner. Throughout the text, I found myself nodding, smiling, amen-ing, and at times wincing at the stark realities. The pain and disappointment so many continue to experience in the church never ceases to grab hold of me and wring my heart. My own journey in Christ is quite similar to Wayne's, in that right after college I experienced a bird's-eye view of the machinations and muddy waters of church leadership. For the better part of twenty years, my husband and I functioned in various traditional church leadership roles, and while we surely met and related to some fantastic people, the leader-driven, vision-based life in the church could not be sustained. Sure, we saw ourselves as "servant leaders," and we tried to live it in purity and grace. But like so many others discovered before us, servant leadership did not lead to the joy and peace one would expect from being a part of a People walking with the Lamb. Sadness over the jockeying for position, competitive spirit, and ongoing frustration-wonderment at the 80 percent of non-functioning congregants led us on a different road, one that was off the beaten path. We sometimes refer to that period of our journey as our desert days. While it was full of dry bones and disillusionment, it wasn't long before the deep wells of living water began to bubble up through the sand. And it was there, right smack in the center of that lonely season, that we learned how living in everyday dependence on the Lord for fellowship, provision, and life could open up many God-moments—opportunities to love and walk with others in much greater closeness and authenticity than living in the frustration of trying to rally a small group to action.

One of the most delightful things about this book is Wayne's ability to wear his heart on his sleeve. While he clearly sees a non-programmatic, informal church functioning in the earth as preferable, there isn't even one point where institutional bashing comes into play. It is rare to find that kind of respect coupled with the conviction he holds. He is unafraid to expose his own frailties and tells stories about the many times that he learned something new in conversation with others. This reveals another of the strengths of this book: the multitude of stories told. We all have stories of our journey—stories that narrate our lives. Jesus was the master of this medium, sharing stories from which generations have gleaned food to nourish our souls. Throughout the book Wayne shares stories from around the world, including his own. I, too, am happy to give you a slice of my own story:

As a teenager I came into the fold toward the end of the Jesus Movement and almost instantly learned how refreshing it is to fellowship with others of like mind. We gathered and sang, shared and worked side by side, growing in knowledge and grace through informal community. No one was in charge of us. We loved Jesus and looked to Him to lead us, and it worked. Through it, I learned straightaway that the church is not an organization, but rather a living, breathing organism, pulsing with the life of the Son of God. Instead of dealing with this truth as an abstract idea, I thought it should be a lived reality and shared it openly. My undoing came with the realization that so many others "leading" the flock of Christ did not really believe this. It's funny how truths of the Kingdom can be so easily obscured by trying to fit in, be the obedient, man-pleasing, doting disciple who all of a sudden is seen as a threat. Funny, but sad. Nonetheless, my own "finding church" became a journey to regain the simplicity and purity of what I experienced in Christ prior to becoming a church leader. Thus, it is particularly joyful to read the stories of so many who are on the same road.

As you set out reading, undoubtedly you will find your own particular points of joy, growth, and resonance, but to my mind, the strength of this book is two-fold. First, and perhaps the most significant, Wayne has undertaken the task of helping readers to see the church as God sees it. We need new eyes—eyes enlivened and renewed by the Holy Spirit—to see what God sees. Toward that end, there is much help in the pages that follow. Second, this book is full of hope. It might just be the holy fire needed to inspire a generation of believers worn out by the unfulfilled promises and potential of the church—the kindling needed for the family of God in the twenty-first century.

And so, dear reader, I leave you with a prayer—one that's taken me through many years of faith, doubt, desperation, and back again to believe that the promises of God for His People are true and REAL. With Paul, I pray that "the God of our Lord Jesus Christ, the Father of glory, may give to you the spirit of wisdom and revelation in the knowledge of Him, the eyes of your understanding being enlightened; that you may know what is the hope of His calling, what are the riches of the glory of His inheritance in the saints, and what is the exceeding greatness of His power toward us who believe." (Ephesians 1:17–19 NKJV)

I believe in God, the Father Almighty and His Son, who came in the flesh and suffered in our stead.

I believe in the Body of Christ—the family that is God's answer to human misery. I believe it is His plan for human flourishing.

So hey—let's not wait 'til heaven to relate!

STEPHANIE BENNETT, author of the Within the Walls trilogy and
Communicating Love: Staying Close in a 24/7 Media-Saturated Society
West Palm Beach, Florida

1 She's Alive and Well

He has also set eternity in the hearts of men;
yet they cannot fathom what God has done
from beginning to end.

ECCLESIASTES 3:11

On my first trip to Israel, the small tour I was with spent an hour in a private part of the Garden of Gethsemane that was open only by appointment. Once inside the walls and away from the crowds we were transported to another time. As we meandered through two-thousand-year-old olive trees, I felt I was inside one of the few places in Israel that carried the weight of authenticity back to the time of Christ. We eventually gathered on a large boulder in the back and, while facing Temple Mount, we contemplated what Jesus had accomplished on the cross.

Imagine my joy when taking my wife there seventeen years later! She wasn't on the first tour and I couldn't wait to share the rustic ambiance of this Garden with her. When we arrived on our last day, I was nearly bursting with anticipation; however, as we walked through the gate, I knew something had gone horribly wrong. Stone-lined pathways cut through the garden. Stacks of outdoor chairs littered the grounds. I hurried to the back of the garden in search of the boulder and could not find it. In its place stood a large, elevated stone patio with amphitheater seating for 100 people all facing a huge lectern stuck on a metal pole. My heart sank as confusion set in. This couldn't be the same garden.

I sought out our tour representative and asked him about the garden I had been in last time. He looked at me, puzzled. What happened to the big rock in back? He had only been working with the tour company for a few years and had never seen it. He assured me this was the same garden I had been in seventeen years before. The boulder (could it have been *that* boulder?) had been buried under the patio. This rustic garden had been turned into a lecture hall, making it more useful to tourists while destroying the purpose for which they'd come.

It was supposed to be so much better than this.

I've had that same feeling about Christianity from my youngest days. First as a follower of Christ, then as a vocational pastor. Don't get me wrong—there were some awesome times in the congregations in which I was involved in my first forty years. But those moments proved more fleeting than I'd hoped, and the fruit far more temporary than it ought.

Is this all there is?

The thought emerged in times of frustration about some conflict or flawed program. But those weren't the only times. Even when things were going well by any external measure, in the quiet place away from the frenetic pace the nagging thought would surface: *There must be something more.*

Have you had similar thoughts? I know few people who haven't, including pastors of some outwardly successful congregations. We were promised a vital relationship with God and the joy of sharing oneness and fellowship with his people, but instead we ended up with a set of disciplines, a weekly service to attend, and a set of rules to follow. And while those might be helpful for a season, somewhere along the line you just feel like something is missing. When Jesus talked about living water flowing from deep within us, or Paul referring to the church as a bride without spot or wrinkle, it made me wonder if I'd missed out somehow.

Had someone covered up the real thing to make it more

palatable to the masses? I looked everywhere and tried so many new ideas to seek the richness of his life that would endure the toughest of times, but always came up short. Often I tried to talk myself out of that hunger, to settle for the fact that Jesus and Paul must have been talking about spiritual realities, not practical ones. But the feeling would return. *There must be something more.*

That thought would drive me for twenty of my adult years, alternating between seasons of working hard to find that something more, and the frustration of watching my latest hope fall short yet again. I used to open talks at pastor seminars with a brief quiz. "Jesus said he would build his church and the gates of Hades would not overcome it. He's been at it now for two thousand years, how do you think he's doing?" Just watching people process the question was fun.

Some were reticent, thinking it presumptuous of me to even suggest they judge Jesus' work. Others pointed out wonderful things about their congregation that led them to believe he was doing a fine job. Still others saw the church of the twenty-first century as a bit of a divided mess, but they couldn't bring themselves to lay the blame for that on Jesus. Even if they liked their particular congregation or denomination, they had concerns about most others. And everyone knows of congregations with leaders so abusive or extravagant they are an affront to the nature of Jesus as well as an embarrassment to the Gospel. Invariably some would admit that their vision for a genuine community of the redeemed—those who love him and one another in a way that restores the broken, encourages the weak, and demonstrates his glory in a fallen world—has gone unfulfilled.

Some pointed out that Sunday morning is the most divisive time of the week in our culture. Our "churches" divide us racially, economically, and socially. We gather with people who see the world like we do and who prefer the same teaching and style of music. While each congregation has its own people in leadership and claims allegiance to the same God, there is little real collaboration between them. In fact, judgments abound between one group and another. Some are thought too liberal and others too legalistic. They disagree on key doctrines and disregard each other's leadership. Some are autocratic and repressive, while others seem to reject Scriptural teachings in favor of a softer message. Some are stuck in rituals others find boring while some spend ridiculous amounts of money to build facilities that look like shopping malls.

"Church splits" are commonplace when people no longer get along. Most people have endured one and few things are more painful. Those who think God is on their side of any issue can be vicious in their attempts to make others conform or be pushed out. Many of these groups fight political battles that rival anything Machiavelli wrote, as they argue over a building project, a new pastor, or how contemporary the music should be.

People have often told me they have suffered more vitriol at the hands of fellow Christians than they have in family or business. Gossip can be more common than fellowship, and the constant plea for more volunteers or more funds are designed to manipulate people's guilt. No wonder most frequent their fellowship only for an hour or so on Sunday, out of obligation, while they ignore it the rest of the week.

So just how well is Jesus doing after two thousand years?

Since you've picked up this book, I suspect you might have concerns about the church as we know it today, or care deeply for someone who does. Maybe you're an active part of a congregation hoping against hope that something can be done to make it more reflective of Jesus' kingdom. Maybe you've already left your congregation and have given up hope that anything can fulfill your longing for his church. Or, maybe your parents stopped attending the fellowship they raised you in and you're wondering if they've lost their minds.

It is no secret that people are leaving their congregations in droves and have been doing so for more than twenty-five years.

Some estimate as many as thirty-five hundred people leave their congregations every day, causing many to close up or merge with others to survive. We may be witnessing the implosion of Christianity in America that mirrors what happened in Europe during previous centuries.

Our religious institutions are become increasingly irrelevant in the cultural conversation and less essential to the fabric of our society. Religious leaders blame this on the secularization of our culture, brought about as science undermines our spiritual underpinnings while the individual grows more narcissistic and indulgent. But those who have left tell a different story. They say that their religious institutions were too focused on money and power, too judgmental of others, and too hypocritical. Disappointed in flawed leadership, wearied of jumping through hoops and still feeling spiritually empty, trapped in superficial relationships, or disillusioned by unanswered prayers, many end up questioning God's character, if not his existence.

This exodus has caused great concern among religious leaders as they watch the declining statistics of those actively involved in their congregations. Because it is easy to blame people for their lack of commitment and outside forces for seducing them, few pastors are taking an honest look at how the local congregation might be part of the problem. Instead of inviting people into a compelling engagement with God, they have resorted to pressure or manipulation, claiming that their attendance is an obligation and without it people will end up devoured by sin, seduced by false theology, or withered up spiritually. One well-known pastor even wrote in a national publication that those who think the congregation is dying owe it to the rest to come and die with it.

Yet people keep leaving. Some reject both God and the church, having never met a God more real than the failures of the institution they attended. They conclude its failure must be proof that God must be a fantasy and plunge headlong into the excesses of a lost world. While that may sound scary, I've seen many of them find the world's ways just as empty and, like the prodigal in Jesus' story, eventually turn again toward the God who beckons them.

Some leave in search of a better congregation. During the past four decades, many have moved into the big-box mega-churches that replaced smaller congregations at about the same time Walmart ate up local mom and pop shops. These impersonal institutions essentially altered the nature of church life. People no longer sit in services with their friends, but in auditoria filled with strangers focused on the entertainment value of the stage or the benefits a large group can provide. Even these have a big back door, as people get bored with the show and weary of the constant appeals for money.

Others look for smaller alternatives, inviting believers to return to their homes with house church gatherings that are more informal. While they offer the promise of more relationship and participation, they don't always turn out that way. Often they are nothing more than the same congregational system, albeit in a smaller setting. They are easy to start and difficult to sustain, as people feel manipulated by the leadership or bored by the meetings.

The "church" as we know it seems to be dying. What does that say about the job Jesus is doing to build his church? I used to think he was doing a frightful job, though I was careful where I expressed that. Mostly it came out in my frustrated prayers about the complications that arose in the congregations in which I participated. While it's easy to blame the problems on flawed humans, Jesus said the powers of darkness couldn't overcome it, so how can human frailty? Paul, the early apostle, even broadened the scope of that promise, saying Jesus would, "present her to himself as a radiant church, without stain or wrinkle or any other blemish, but holy and blameless." (Ephesians 5:27) That's quite a picture, and it's hard to see that the church of our day is any closer to that reality than the church of Paul's day.

If you share my frustration with the disparity between the

church as Scripture talks about her and what we see reflected in our religious institutions, you're not alone. You're standing in a long line that includes the likes of Francis of Assisi, John Wycliffe, Martin Luther, John Wesley, and nameless others who dared to ask the difficult questions and struggled with the uncomfortable answers.

Just maybe your growing discouragement is not the proof of his failing, but the evidence of his working.

What if he is actually behind this move away from institutionalized Christianity? What if he is inviting people into a simpler and more effective way to express the reality of his family? What if that church has been growing since the Day of Pentecost, and we've missed it—not because it wasn't there but because we were so distracted by human attempts to build our own version of the church that we missed the more glorious one Jesus is building? I know this may be difficult to consider if you've only known the church as the sanctioned institutions that use the label, but it may well be a question worth asking, especially if you no longer feel at home in a local congregation.

Unless we're willing to say Jesus has done a poor job building his church, the question begs us to consider that his church is something different than our human attempts can consistently reflect. What would the church of Jesus Christ look like if it were made up of people who were learning to live in the same reality Jesus did, with an eye on his Father and a compassionate heart for people around him? How well would we love one another and how much would we reflect his glory if we weren't spending so much time and energy attending to our institutions?

That's not an idealistic dream. That church is already taking shape around the world.

To embrace that reality, however, we're going to have to see the church as he does, not how we've been taught to define her. The longing to find a church that fulfills the promise of Scripture is God's gift, drawing you toward a greater reality than you've yet seen. I know how frustrating it can feel when your tastes of it seem to fade like a mirage in the distance, but his church is alive and well. She is not and never has been the building on the corner. Evidence of her may be there, but she's far more glorious than our institutions or denominations could possibly contain.

Finding her has been the quest of my life. I pastored for twenty years hoping to find a congregational system that would allow people to experience his reality. It was only after I was forced out that I began to get a glimpse of the reality I'd been seeking most of my life.

I found her where I least expected her to be—right in front of me! I had been searching for her in all the wrong places and actually had no idea what I was looking for until I stumbled upon her. It was far simpler than I considered, and when I embraced that reality I found myself at home with a family I always hoped existed. Jesus is building this church by quietly bringing together a family so rich and vast that she doesn't need the religious conventions we've used to contain her.

These are the conclusions I've reached in the sixtieth year of my journey. I, too, would have been skeptical of them had I only heard of them from afar and not experienced firsthand the richness and beauty of his church alongside so many others. These observations are not mine alone but the fruit of many conversations with others from all over the world who have struggled with the same questions and come to similar conclusions. They embrace deep fellowship both with Christ and with his church in a way that goes mostly unseen. The friendships we share have profoundly shaped my journey and fulfill every passion I've had to see the body of Christ in all her glory.

None of us would claim to be experts who have it all figured out, but simply passionate people who have witnessed how his church actually takes shape in our world. So now I take up the task of helping others to find her as well, even if you don't yet know that's what you are seeking. What you will find on these pages is what I wish someone would have told me in my teens and saved me forty years of frustration. But honestly, I don't know that I would have listened. The pathway to make my mark on the world and to succeed by my own achievements was too compelling and the road less traveled so uninviting by comparison. It just may be that the only way to find this road is through the frustration of trial and error; that struggle may be as important to participating in the reality of his church as the knowledge itself.

Some of you have already tasted of her splendor but didn't realize what it was because she didn't fit in the box others said she should. Somehow you fell into a circle of friends who were passionate about following Jesus, and you found yourself in conversations that were filled with life and joy. Your friends encouraged your journey as well as gave you the space to struggle with your deeper questions and doubt.

Some of you haven't tasted that yet, but you have an undeniable longing for something more than you've known. You keep trying to fit into the conventional system but something beckons you beyond that, and you're not even sure how to explain it. Your friends and family may not understand and even wonder if you must be crazy. You are not. Something is awakening in you that may bring more frustration than joy at the outset, but if you don't give up and if you don't settle for "the best you can find," that hunger will work in you and eventually you will find her, too.

A number of years ago I was invited to speak at a black, inner-city fellowship near Boston. As I joined their meeting for the evening, I was struck by how passive the people were even as the pastor railed at them for not being as faithful in attendance as she wanted them to be. We went through all the motions. We sang. I spoke, they listened, and while those times are not valueless, they are not what church life is about.

The next morning I met two young men from that congregation for breakfast at their request. As we ate they shared their stories and their spiritual hungers, which were not being met where they were. They talked about the community they lived in and their desire to see a display of Jesus' life available to them. We laughed, we cried, and we prayed, unaware that others were listening to us.

After a couple of hours of conversation, two ladies in their seventies suddenly appeared at the end of our table with tears in their eyes. "You don't know how long we have been praying for God to touch some young men in this community who have a passion to share God's life in such a desperate place. We have enjoyed listening to you three for the past couple of hours and know this is part of the answer to our prayers." We all knew we were in a transcendent moment and right there, if ever so briefly, the church took shape in a restaurant in Roxbury, Massachusetts, and it was far more soul shaping than the meeting we'd had the previous night.

If you've ever been in that kind of moment, no religious activity will ever satisfy again. That's what many people are wandering away from established congregations to find—a city whose builder is God. They are not looking for an unrealistic ideal full of perfect people, but a real community of flawed people who are being shaped by the love of God, and who can share that love together even beyond their imperfections.

For the past twenty years I have enjoyed her in my own engagements at home, but also in varying expressions around the world. She's filled with love and tenderness, resilient in the face of trouble, putting God's kingdom above self-interest, relationship above conformity, compassion above agreement, and freedom above obligation. She expresses a depth of community, joy, and sharing that humans are incapable of producing on their own.

There really is something more, and I want you to enjoy her as much as I have.

2

The Community of a New Creation

I am making everything new!
REVELATION 21:5

I know what they mean, but the language still jars me: "They left the church." Or, "I left the church ten years ago." Since they have continued to passionately follow Jesus, I want to correct them. You may have left your *congregation,* but how did you leave the *church*? Do you think you can belong to him and not be part of his family? It's one of the tragic consequences of using the term to describe the myriad of religious institutions that dot our landscape instead of the tapestry of his people Jesus is weaving together.

When Scripture talks about the church, it does so with a profound sense of wonder as the crowning glory of God's work in human history. In addition to being the spotless bride, unstained by the world, Paul also says she is "his body, the fullness of him who fills everything in every way." (Eph. 1:23) What an incredible picture—a family taking shape in the world that expresses everything he is! None of us could do that on our own, but the synergy of our care and cooperation can replicate his nature and glory. This has been God's desire from the beginning, to bring all things together under one head—to Jesus himself! (Eph. 1:10) That unity of heart and purpose will further display the "manifold wisdom of God...to the rulers and authorities in the heavenly realms." (Eph. 3:10)

As we become more one with him, each of us will reflect a bit of his glory. When we connect with others who are also being shaped by him, we find an immediate oneness and affection as we recognize his life in them. The way we love one another, the unity with which we pray, and the combining of our gifts and resources to do the tasks he gives us to do will reveal his nature not only to people around us, but will actually undermine the unseen spiritual forces that seek to destroy humanity.

Anyone who beats with God's heart yearns to engage this family. Granted, you may not have seen that reality in the groups you have been part of in the past, but that doesn't mean she doesn't exist. This community is growing to trust him and the way he works, and they are learning the simple joy of living in the Father's affection and sharing it with others. You'll find it where people lay down their lives for each other, where they don't fight to be first or thought more spiritual, and where they would rather be defrauded than push for their own way. As they relate together under his leading, this church is the most exciting, functional family ever!

If we start there, then our conventional definition of the church as a religious institution is unworkable. How could it ever produce such a thing? A group doesn't take on that reality simply because it calls itself a church. We have attached the word that was meant to unveil the glory of Father's family to institutions that are incapable of reflecting it for any sustained period. That's why when we use the word *church* for any collection of people who self-identify as Christians, we miss that reality. They may do many of the things we'd expect a church to do—teach the Gospel, encourage fellowship, and reach out to the lost—but they begin by staking out their beliefs by forcing a meeting structure, decision-making process, and their mission. They try to make people good Christians by getting them to conform to those plans and expectations with varying degrees of pressure and varying degrees of success. The fact that we have hundreds of thousands of such groups all claiming to be the church and that they have so little in common renders the term meaningless.

Jesus' church is not a human creation. Rather, it is the fruit of the relationships of those who are part of a new creation—the redeemed race of humanity that relates to him as the Head. When Paul tells us that the church is the fullness of Christ, he's moving beyond a collection of Christians and talking about a vibrant community that lives at his pleasure and as his complement in the world. The church Jesus is building has been growing since the day he inaugurated it at Pentecost. It is not a meeting or an institution *per se*, but a growing family. It takes shape wherever people who are engaged with him interact with one another. Rather than thinking of it as a group to join, it might be better to look for that reality in the conversations, connections, and collaborations he gives us each day. As you will see, it can appear almost anywhere at any time.

"Wherever two or three who are following Jesus are together you have a functioning church." I nearly fell out of my pew the first time I heard that. It came out of the mouth of the senior pastor of the first staff position I'd ever held while he was teaching through Matthew 18. I'm not sure he believed it given his focus on commitment and accountability to the institution he led. I didn't either at the time. But I think Jesus does, and that's why when this twenty-four-year-old associate pastor heard it, his heart soared. What if it is true, and what if it provides a better understanding of the church than the one most of us have been given?

The church of the new creation is more like wildflowers strewn across an alpine meadow than a walled garden with manicured hedges. I realize such a seemingly amorphous view of the church will make many nervous, especially those who think it their God-given duty to manage a group of people on his behalf or else the church can't exist. But it can. And I'm not advocating for the isolated, everyone-is-a-church-to-themselves idea. The church takes her expression in relationships we have with others who are also following him—local friendships as well as international connections that he knits together. We'll first see it reflected in conversations where Jesus makes himself known. Some of those conversations will grow into more enduring friendships that become part of the fabric of our lives as we serve, encourage, and grow together. These friendships will lead to others, and out of that network of friends and friends of friends, God will have all the resources he needs to invite us to agreement in prayer and collaborative actions to fulfill his purposes around us.

Can it really be that simple? This is perhaps the greatest stumbling block to people seeing the church for what she is. It's too simple, they think, or too easy. So they put their trust in the vast array of discordant institutions instead of the work of Jesus. As we'll see connecting is difficult only because it is far easier than we dare to believe. In fact, you probably have those growing connections with people, even in the congregation you attend. I'm only suggesting that your interaction with them expresses more freely the life of the church than sitting in a pew watching the staged activity up front.

Admittedly this discussion about church is not easy to have. Most people want simple, clear answers to heavily nuanced realities. It would be easier to say that all religious institutions are bad, and smaller, more informal groups are good, except that it isn't true. If we just had an organization that represented the one, true church led by the right people then we would know who is in and who is out, except that every group who has ever tried it has ended up arrogant and abusive in trying to keep it pure.

So we are going to have to make a distinction in our minds between the church that humanity has attempted to build for two thousand years, and the community of the new creation that Jesus is building. They are not the same, though they can gloriously overlap on occasion. It's just that our conformity-based structures cannot produce the internal transformation necessary for the church to take shape among us. And as much as we have to see how our congregational doctrines, rituals, and structures can fail us, I'm not saying they are evil. This isn't a matter of whether these are good or bad, but how we use them. If they enhance our growing relationship with God, great! It's when they become a substitute for the relationship we lack that they are problematic.

I agree with the theology of the historic creeds and reading them inspires me. It is not our mental assent that's important, however, but living inside the truth they espouse. Likewise, ritual can open our hearts into a wider world and help us reflect on him, or it can become meaningless repetition that only makes us feel more distant from the Living God. I'm not against structure, which is incredibly valuable whenever it gives shape to what Jesus is doing among a group of people. Everything I do has structure, from the books I publish, to the travel I arrange, to our work in Africa with orphans and widows. Structure is essential to coordinate people to accomplish specific tasks, but history shows us that no group structure can successfully reflect the life of Jesus' church for very long. It happens subtly but, over time, people end up serving the structure. They become dependent on it, instead of following him.

In the end, however, no creed, ritual, or structure can contain the church Jesus is building. And strangely enough, neither do any of those things exclude the possibility of the church taking shape. Because the church takes expression wherever people are learning to live alongside Jesus in the new creation, it can appear almost anywhere. It's a family, and that family is defined by the nature of their relationships of love to one another.

Years ago a friend offered me a challenge. "Why don't we only use the term *church* the way Paul talks about her in the Scriptures? Let's call the church what he calls the church and not be distracted by the institutions that use the term for something less than that reality." It hasn't been easy. Common usage trips me up all the time, but I do think the word is worth preserving as a term of endearment so that as we read the Scriptures it will evoke the church Jesus had in mind. I'm going to endeavor to do that here. Rather than use the term for any collection of Christians that meet together in an established system, I'll use the term *church* to describe the family of God that Jesus is putting on display. When I talk about institutions, I'm going to use the words *congregation* or *fellowship*. When, because of popular usage, I have no choice but to use the word "church" (such as "church split") for that which is not truly the church, I'll set it off with quotes.

For the past twenty years, I have been privileged to be part of a growing conversation with people all over the world who are losing their confidence that an institution can provide the environment the church of Jesus Christ needs to flourish. Some of us have already left institutionalized Christianity either because we were pushed out for asking the wrong questions or because we could no longer continue to serve the demands of an institution that seemed so at odds with the passion growing in our hearts. None of us did so easily, having spent decades serving in local congregations and engaged in multiple efforts to reform them. In the end we left not to abandon our faith, but to explore that faith on a more vibrant journey than those structures would allow.

Many others share the same concerns but are still engaged institutionally either because they are hopeful of finding an institutional solution or because they are simply making the best of a system for which they see no plausible alternative. Many of these are pastors and elders who know better than anyone else the constant struggle between institutional needs and living the priorities of Jesus' kingdom. Others stay for fear of being alienated from family and friends.

To be clear, I am not writing this book for those who are comfortable in the institutions we've inherited in the twenty-first century, but for those who have the nagging feeling that there must be something more than "church," as we've come to know it. If you are hoping I'll give people ten reasons why they have to go to a local congregation, you will be disappointed. If you're looking for me to condemn the well-intended people who are trying to make our religious institutions work as well as they can, I won't do that either. While I'm convinced that no system can replicate the life of the church among a group of people, I have seen the reality of his church expressed in relationships there as well. If you're looking for a how-to guide so you can build a better model of the church where you live, you might as well stop reading here. You're about to discover that it is not your job, and your best efforts can't replicate it. Finally, if you hoped for a "church-bashing" book, you won't find it here. I love the church Jesus is building, this amazing network of people who are learning to live in him. I've seen expressions of her almost everywhere—in a chance encounter on a plane, in a conversation with a neighbor, with a network of friends who live near me, or collaborating on a project with gracious and generous people.

It will not help us to split into adversarial groups, one that champions the local congregation and one that condemns it. Hasn't there been enough division in this family over things that don't truly matter? My hope for the church includes them both, because in the end it isn't about the meetings we attend or avoid, but whether we are coming alive in his kingdom and sharing that life with others in whatever format he places us. Wouldn't it serve the purposes of Jesus more if we could reach beyond the places and people we prefer to embrace the expression of his family however she makes herself known?

Where we begin, however, is not by trying to fix our congregations, but looking toward our own awakening inside a new creation. This is where church life begins and the only environment in which the church can take shape. I don't think any of us can yet conceive of what his church will look like when thousands upon thousands of people freely live in the reality of Jesus' love and respond to the voice of the Shepherd simultaneously and spontaneously around the world.

3 | The Awakening

The water I give will become a spring of
water welling up to eternal life.

JOHN 4:14

It took me more than thirty years to wake up to the reality of the new creation that Jesus first planted in my heart at nine years of age. It certainly didn't need to take so long and I hope what I have learned will help others shorten that time significantly.

As my heart awakened to his reality, I was quickly pushed onto the performance treadmill of religious obligation. I found I could work it well, even though it never fulfilled the longing of my heart. Whenever God tried to nudge me to a different reality, I resisted, not realizing what I was doing or what other course to try. So I suppressed those inklings and ran even harder on the treadmill, hoping against hope that some day it would work.

For those of us steeped in religious performance, the moments when we know it isn't working can be incredibly confusing. Looking back now, I know it was the new creation awakening in me pushing against the religious obligations I was trained to revere. Like a seedling pushing past the rocks and through the soil, his growing life was reaching for the surface. Though it took many years, in the end it won out when I stopped embracing Christianity as a religion of rituals and rules and started embracing Christ himself. All along he was inviting me to live beyond the elementary principles of this world—inside the new creation Jesus had inserted inside the old. Discovering his life meant I had to learn an entirely different way to live.

I was a company man from the beginning, certain that the system we'd inherited from two thousand years of Christian history was the extension of what Scripture referred to as the church. I grew up in the blessings and confines of congregational life. Sure, it had its flaws and some congregations were better reflections of his kingdom than others, but we had nothing else, or so I thought. While I never sought out a perfect church, I did want one that at least aspired to the ideals of its Founder by facilitating an environment where people would grow to know God and share his life together with honesty, generosity, and compassion.

I had every hope that the flaws of congregational life could be reformed, its priorities righted, and its mission revitalized. That hope formed the content of many conversations and conferences and filled my library with books offering ideas for renewal. For twenty years of professional ministry, I gave myself to reformation as a vocational pastor and as a contributing editor to *Leadership Journal*. My first book, *The Naked Church*, expressed my hope for a systemic change in our church experience.

That experience began in the earliest weeks of life, in the nursery of the First Baptist Church of Selma, California, where my parents were deeply involved. I grew up believing that God dwelled in that sanctuary in the same way he lived in the tabernacle of Israel, and that was not always a comforting thought. At the same time, however, I was captured by the stories of Jesus and the invitation to have a relationship with him. While we had great times with close friends, our official activities were more boring than compelling. We attended out of a sense of duty to God and fear that failure to do so might negatively impact our well being either here or in the afterlife.

In my preteen years, my parents got involved in a renewal

just beginning to make inroads into California. It didn't have a name yet, but offered a connection with God's Spirit as an active presence, empowering us beyond our abilities and helping us discern God's voice. Initially our Baptist congregation was open to this renewal, but it didn't take long before pride and ignorance divided those who had a "fresh infilling" of the Spirit from those who didn't. The leadership eventually concluded that those who claimed to hear from God were at best deluded and at worst demon-possessed. Lifelong friends were soon divided over the controversy, and those who embraced the renewal were forced out to form their own congregation. But that, too, was short-lived, as controversies arose about how much expression of the Spirit in our Sunday gatherings would enhance God's work among us, and how much of it would offend visitors. It didn't take long for this group of friends to split again.

For the next few years my family drifted through some smaller churches and even formed our own house church for one stretch. While our connections with others deepened during these days, as did our knowledge of God and his ways, there were always major problems lurking just beneath the surface. Everything we tried was tainted by man's efforts and failures. Gossip and conflict divided people, and most of those who aspired to lead us during those various groups evidenced serious character flaws leading to sordid affairs, both sexual and financial. I found it disheartening that one could know so much about Jesus without being shaped by his life.

Though I wouldn't express it in the same way today, it was during this time that I felt "called to the ministry" and garnered admiration for choosing such a noble pursuit. That heady brew would prove to be quite a trap in days to come. But following my sense at the time, I ended up in Biblical studies at Oral Roberts University in the early '70s, as the Charismatic renewal was being corrupted by those who sought to establish their authority over the movement and by those who taught that we could manipulate

God for our own prosperity. Our required chapels offered quite a contrast to more spiritually engaging relationship that grew among the students and whetted my appetite for a deeply transforming life in Jesus. I met a great many with a passion for Jesus, including a young Ohio woman who would become my wife.

Upon graduation I was offered a staff position in a growing congregation where I had grown up. I was excited to get the offer since I admired the pastor and appreciated what that congregation stood for in that city. But within a few years it became clear that we were talking about realities we weren't truly experiencing, at least in the formal activities of the congregation. We talked about being a family, but real relationships were undermined by a controlling system that encouraged people to follow the pastor instead of following Jesus. We hoped the former would produce the latter, but it never turned out that way. Most parishioners were too dependent on the program and the staff to explore their own spiritual journey.

When I had an opportunity to move fifty miles south and help with a new "church" plant, I took it. With all the "humility" my twenty-seven years of age could muster, I was off to implement my view of a relational community that I hoped would offer a better reflection of his church. Though we offered a Sunday morning celebration, our midweek home groups would be the real touchstone of our life together. We learned some amazing things about God, helped people grow in their own relationship, and facilitated friendships that became lifelong treasures. But once again the joy of relationship gave way to the pressing demands of our growing institution, and conflict arose when diverse agendas wanted to control the resources God had given us. After fifteen years, my best friend and co-pastor announced my resignation, which I had not offered, one Sunday morning while I was out of town.

I returned to expose the lie and take back control, which I had both the authority and popularity to do. As the week wore on, however, I had a sense that God had more to teach me if I walked away than if I stayed. It was the hardest decision I ever made. I couldn't believe that our little experiment to do church more relationally would turn out like so many others, shipwrecked by human ambition. So in my early forties, exiled from the congregation I had helped to shape, my life took a different trajectory. For a few years I searched some other alternatives—like house church, which was a rising hope for many in that day—but nothing offered any meaningful alternative to what I'd already tried. Eventually I gave up looking.

I hadn't given up on Jesus, however, nor had many of my friends. We began to discover how deeply loved by God we were, and that some of what we had been taught in the Christian religion, especially as it played out in congregational life, was at odds with that reality.

Instead of seeking a church structure that could sustain the kind of community my heart longed for, I gave up and simply started to follow what God was unfolding in my heart. Yes, I was accused of being bitter, independent, and rebellious, but I was far from bitter. I was certain that I was not wired to fulfill the cultural role of a vocational pastor, and I walked away in hopes of uncovering something else. Neither was I independent; I had lots of friendships and a deep thirst to find authentic community. I might have been rebellious, but certainly not toward God, only toward the religious structures that seemed to undermine his work.

A few years into that process a close friend asked me why I was no longer talking as much about the church as I had before. I remember responding, "I've spent the last twenty years thinking, scheming, and tweaking my ideas about church. I've only had a couple of years now to learn what it truly means to live inside the affection of the Father and to follow Jesus with a growing trust in him. I am going to enjoy this for a while and may not get back to considering what church might look like for another decade."

It turned out to be a bit longer than that. But a funny thing happened in the meantime: By simply following what Jesus put on my heart and loving people around me, I found myself living squarely in the middle of the church life I had been hungering for all those years. I didn't even realize it at first, because it didn't fit into one of the sanctioned boxes I thought to be essential to identify as a church. There were no services, no buildings, no committee meetings, no designated leaders, no permanence, and no name in which to stake our identity. Those who knew Jesus best around me had no desire to create institutions or set themselves up as its leaders, preferring to care for others in need and helping them learn to follow him.

I ended up with vibrant connections to other people who were also learning to live the life of Jesus. We were having conversations that stimulated us to live more deeply and gatherings that were rich and encouraging. We even collaborated on tasks Jesus seemed to nudge us toward with great joy and fruitfulness. We didn't feel the need to create formal attachments or press ourselves into weekly meetings.

That's when my view of the church shifted. I had been looking for her in structures and organizations, but they always seemed to gravitate away from the substance I was looking for. I began to see it in a growing network of people who are being transformed by the love of God. They are warm, engaging, kind, generous, and passionate. They allow people to be honest even about their doubts, struggles, and failures. They free people from shame, not exploit it for their own ends, and they will encourage you away from the bondage of religious obligation that has little impact on how you live your life with Jesus.

I'd been living in the church most of my life without recognizing her because I was so busy trying to create a version of my own. I'd tasted of her reality in the closer friendships of virtually every congregation I'd ever attended, but because this wasn't part of the official program I didn't see them as the church. It was a classic case of missing the forest for the trees and explained why we allowed the needs of the program to displace those friendships.

I then realized that the longing that had brought me so much frustration in that environment was simply the result of him awakening me into a new creation. Perhaps that's what you're experiencing as well, caught between a growing desire to live freely in his affection, and the confusion of our human systems that do more to undermine that desire than fulfill it. Now I know that this new creation could never be contained in a human organization. She may exist alongside it, but she transcends it in the same way Jesus transcends the old creation.

The church Jesus builds is a family living in the growing reality of his affection. That's why Jesus said he would build his church because we are not capable of doing so and our attempts have always distorted her image and hurt others in the process in spite of whatever good they have done. Jesus established his church by inaugurating a new creation of men and women who would live beyond the human conventions of society. It can only be expressed in the interaction of lives he is transforming.

His church does not arise from the old creation and thus will defy all our attempts to contain it or manage it. His church is a reality we recognize as our relationship with him grows. Our task was never to build it, but only to give ourselves to the new creation and watch as his church takes shape around us as he links our lives with others. We don't have to name it or try to control it, but simply cooperate with her as long as she takes expression around us. When it has served its purpose we can let go of that expression to see what he will do next. The relationships endure, not necessarily the task or the program that gave it shape.

There is more in the Gospels to commend this view of church than anything that points us to the religious systems we have since created. Jesus was quite clear about the nature of his church, we just missed it because we never considered that he told us everything he wanted us to know about the church.

4 | What Jesus Taught Us

The work of God is this: to believe in the one
he has sent.

JOHN 6:29

Y ou can't read the Gospels without realizing that Jesus was not
as preoccupied with the church as we are today.

As far as we know, he didn't teach his disciples how to plant
them, build them, or manage them. He didn't hold any leadership
training conferences, give them a workbook with all they needed
to know safely tucked inside, or even start a seminary. He didn't
show them how to form and manage a nonprofit organization. He
didn't teach them how to hold a service, to lead worship, to exegete
an Old Testament passage, or even to write the New Testament.

He didn't craft a doctrine statement so they would know true
believers from fake ones. He didn't give them seminars on small
group fellowship, organizing a leadership team, or planning an
evangelistic outreach. Instead he simply walked through life,
touching people he met, showing them the reality of his Father's
kingdom, and inviting them to live in it. He wasn't ever in a
meeting that looked like our Sunday services. In fact he didn't
seem to do one thing that would have prepared his disciples
to hold a congregational service or organize an international
organization to sustain the life of his followers.

Of course, just because he didn't do those things doesn't mean we can't. But it might make us wonder about their value or at least question the idea that you can't be part of his church if you're not involved with a group of people doing those things. Jesus didn't talk much about the church at all, mentioning it only twice. He said simply that he would build it and he gave some counsel about dealing with someone who is wittingly or unwittingly destroying it.

It doesn't seem like much, does it? Even at that, what if he told us, and more importantly showed us, everything we needed to know about his church?

The assumption, of course, is that he didn't. That's why most seminars about church life turn to a few verses from Paul, or worse yet Moses' leadership over the tribes of Israel. While Paul does talk about the church often, and writes to the church in various localities to address problems in or to answer questions about their shared life, Paul didn't seem to do any more of those things we identify with church today than Jesus did. We never see him in a Sunday service with a worship team or as a Bible lecturer. He certainly would never have conceived of multiple "churches" in the same city having different names, different doctrines, and different "worship styles." They didn't have ruling boards to make decisions or buildings to gather in, other than their own homes.

So when we quote Scriptures and apply them as justification for whatever we might be doing at the Whoville Community Church, we miss the point entirely. Our way of organizing congregations in the twenty-first century has little in Scripture to commend it. We spend more time making the Scriptures fit our preconceived view of church, rather than deriving our understanding of church from the Scriptures themselves.

Our view of "church life" today has far more to do with institutional identity, meetings, rituals, ethics, and doctrines than demonstrating what a community of Godly love looks like. From that foundation, it is difficult to find our way into the reality of Christ's church. Maybe he didn't talk so much about the church because it was not the means to his end. What if he knew it was simply the fruit of his working and that it takes shape quite easily wherever people learn to follow him?

If so, then Jesus really did tell us everything we needed to know about the church by *not* talking about it. His entire ministry was focused on a kingdom that he was inaugurating. Like the beachhead at Normandy, he invaded this broken world to insert the life of God into human history. He embodied that kingdom, spoke about it in parables, and invited people to embrace it by embracing him. Matthew, Mark, and Luke use the term "kingdom" more than one hundred times in their recollections of Jesus and what was important to him.

The terminology switches in John. He uses the term *kingdom* sparingly, but uses the words *life* and *eternal life* to talk about the same reality. For John, *eternal life* didn't just describe life after death, but the quality of God's life that we can experience now by entering into an affection-based relationship with Father, Son, and Spirit. Jesus opened the door for us to participate in the divine community in the midst of this broken creation.

The Jews of the first century made the mistake of assuming that the kingdom of the Messiah would be a political kingdom that would overthrow Rome and lead them to prosperity. Disillusioned when Jesus indicated no passion to do so, they rejected him. They sought a physical kingdom, and they couldn't see the more powerful kingdom that was making its way into the world through Jesus himself. Proclaiming freedom, offering forgiveness, healing the sick, loving the outcast, and making his home among fallen humanity were signs that the kingdom had already come. Rather than shape our political world, it would transform a new race of men and women to live inside the reality of God in the chaos of a fallen planet. By dancing to a different melody than the self-preferring strains of the world, they would reveal God's love to a world in desperate need of it.

But Christianity has made the same mistake the first-century

Jewish leaders did, by confusing a spiritual kingdom with political power. Christians have taken two oft-traveled roads here, either by trying to employ the political and economic powers of the old creation to conform society to their liking, or by simply waiting until the end of the age when Jesus subdues all powers. They still see the kingdom in a material sense and frame their view of church accordingly. But in doing so, they miss the true nature of the kingdom, the new creation, and the church.

The realm of Jesus' kingdom lies in the human heart. Its currency is not political or economic power, but lives transformed by love, embracing a different set of priorities and a different mission. So despite what Jesus did or didn't say to his disciples about the church, he did teach them the power of love and he challenged them to share as freely with the world what love they had received from him. The life of the new creation flows from the Father's affection.

The best presentation of the Gospel I ever heard came out of the mouth of an atheist, who hated Christians. That was his description of himself in the opening moments of our conversation on a flight from Los Angeles to Pittsburgh. I understood his angst, especially in light of the *Time* magazine cover story he was reading about the heated culture war issues that has divided our nation. A few moments later, he asked me what I did for a living.

I told him that was not an easy question to answer. I haven't had normal job responsibilities for some time. On any given day I could be writing, traveling, speaking, counseling, or even consulting with public schools on religious liberty issues. So I often answer that question by the answer I gave him: "I wander around the planet helping people sort out what Jesus really taught."

"Oh you do, do you?" he responded with an amused chuckle in his voice. And then he asked me the same question that almost everyone asks me when I introduce myself that way. "Do you know what I think Jesus taught?"

That response used to surprise me, thinking they would want

to know what I thought. But, no, they want to tell me what they think. So, here a self-professed atheist who hates Christians is going to tell me what Jesus really taught. And that's exactly where I want the conversation to begin. I would learn a lot by his next few words. I have heard many people tell me what they think Jesus really taught and they are often wrong, sometimes even hilarious. Not this time. What came out of this man's mouth shocked me.

"I think Jesus taught us that we have a Father who loves us more than we know, and if we could sort that out we would know how to treat each other."

My jaw dropped open. Held speechless for a moment, it was his turn to look into my amazed countenance. "What?" he asked.

"I've never heard it put better," I responded with a shake of my head.

"Really?"

"Yes, really! I've heard the Gospel presented by some of the most famous preachers of our day and read about it in books of those who came before. I have never heard it expressed better by any of them."

"Where did you get that?" I asked, thinking he must have heard it in an old Sunday school class somewhere. But he shrugged as if he had no idea.

"Do you know that's exactly what Jesus said?"

"He did?"

"Yes, in John 13. 'A new command I give you: Love one another. As I have loved you, so you must love one another. By this all men will know that you are my disciples, if you love one another.' Yours is a pretty good version of that statement. So tell me, why don't you believe it?"

"I've never seen it lived." I could feel the pain in his words.

"I have," I told him, and he wanted to know more. For the next hour and a half, I told him about people I know who have been so deeply transformed by the Father's love that they have given themselves away to help others, even to those who had misused or betrayed them. They did it not because they had to, but because the affection they had in their heart wouldn't let them do otherwise.

In the end, he was deeply touched and I told him that the Gospel had already been planted in his heart. He might want to reconsider what it means to follow Jesus. He assured me he would.

The power of Jesus' kind of love is infectious. Who doesn't want to be the object of someone else's affection, especially if that person wants nothing in return? That's how God's love differs from lesser human versions of it. We mostly talk of love as the mutual accommodation of self-need. As long as you provide something valuable for me and I provide something valuable for you, we can say we love each other. So our version of love is exploitive from the beginning. It's based on what I can get from someone else and they me. If that mutual benefit is interrupted in some way, or if people ask for more than we have to give, the relationship dies.

Jesus defined love not by what we can get, but by what we give. "Greater love has no one than this, that he lay down his life for his friends." For Jesus, love was a reality, not a commitment. He wasn't committed to us; he genuinely cared enough for us that laying down his life was his only choice in the face of our brokenness. Love is never what we have to do for someone; it's what we want to do to help someone we care deeply about.

That's why love had to begin inside of God. We hadn't a clue what it was until he showed us. It is a relational connection that seeks the good of another above our own. Jesus didn't just talk about it; he demonstrated it—in the way he treated people, even sinners, and in his willingness to make the ultimate sacrifice to break the cycle of destructiveness in the world and free us from our own self-preferring nature.

His kingdom is not a political system nor can it be contained in a religious one. It is a vast network of people, well loved by the Father and, thus, loving others well. That would be enough, he said, for the whole world to come to know who he is. So, what if when he was walking the countryside with his disciples, talking to a woman at a well, sitting in Zaccheus's home having lunch, or relaxing in Bethany, he was showing us exactly what his church looks like?

So when Jesus spent time with the Samaritan woman at a well, told the story of the Good Samaritan, or embraced Peter with prayer *before* and love *after* his betrayal, he was showing us how the church lives.

Maybe he did after all tell us everything we needed to know about his church. Its teaching is more like a conversation about faith in the stern of a boat after a fierce storm than it is a lecture from a pulpit with a PowerPoint presentation looming in the background. Its gatherings look more like a meal in the upper room than people sitting in rows of pews or theater seats. And its leadership is better expressed in washing dirty feet than sitting in a council meeting fighting over the budget.

One thing is sure, the heritage Jesus left us is a far better reflection of God's reality than the two thousand years we've spent fighting over doctrine, building cathedrals, fine-tuning our programs and policies, and arrogantly trying to claim our stake of power in the structures of the world. Even though the church that humanity has built has helped spread the message of the Gospel throughout the world, it has done so at an exorbitant cost.

5 | What Our History Has Confirmed

... having a form of Godliness but denying its power.

2 TIMOTHY 3:5

"The closer I get to Jesus, the harder it is to pastor this congregation."

What a surprising statement from a young man riding the crest of a swelling congregation that would be the envy of many.

When I asked what he meant, he continued. "When I am close to him, I can't treat these people the way I need to for all this to work." He nodded toward the huge building complex in which we were standing. While he had yet to concede that there wasn't an answer that was still eluding him, he couldn't have described better the conundrum of living the priorities of Jesus while trying to manage an institution. I had felt that same conflict almost daily in the twenty years I was employed as a pastor.

Jesus had it easy. Because he didn't have to run a ministry or manage a congregation, he was free to engage people exactly as he found them. He didn't have to make them do anything for him; thus, he was free to love them and they were free to respond to that love or reject it. He didn't need their tithes to pay his salary, their attendance to validate his ego, or their time to fill out his program.

Maybe he was on to something. Whenever we move from sharing the kingdom freely to managing people for their own good, a host of harmful things can result even with our best intentions. That's how we traded a kingdom of love for a religion of rituals, creeds, rules, and icons, and how its leaders became those who manage programs instead of helping people live in relationship with a loving Father.

As we look back over Christian history, we see an unrelenting trend that moves away from the purity and simplicity of devotion to Jesus toward a dependence on religious institutions and those who run them. Even while the Scriptures were still being penned, it was obvious that the early believers found it easier to trust systems to manage people's behavior than to help them discover transformative relationships with Jesus. There didn't seem to be a need to manage the three thousand new followers in Jerusalem after Pentecost. It appears they quite easily found themselves at the temple where the disciples were explaining the life and message of Jesus, and their homes filled with fellowship, prayer, eating together, and generosity as they gave sacrificially to those in need.

Then someone came up with the idea of laying the money at the apostle's feet instead of giving directly to those in need. That opened a trap door wide enough for Ananias and Sapphira to fall through. They tried to game that system by claiming an offering larger than they gave so others would think them more spiritual. But they weren't the only ones caught in the trap. It seems to me the apostles got caught as well.

When a dispute broke out between the Jews from Israel and those from Greece over equitable distribution of food to their widows, the disciples tried to remove themselves claiming they had weightier matters to deal with. So they appointed seven men to take responsibility for the problem while they set themselves aside for "prayer and the ministry of the Word." Isn't it interesting how the focus of Acts then shifts away from the apostles to two of those who had been chosen to distribute the funds? Stephen gets stoned for his witness in Jerusalem, and Phillip starts a revival in Samaria. Where are the apostles? Evidently they were still in their prayer closets and studies missing the action. Finally Peter and John go to Samaria to see if they can help Phillip.

I wonder if Luke told this story not as a positive example of dealing with need, but as a warning against institutional fixes to relational problems. Far from being proof of centralized offerings, isn't it more likely a warning that when they did so it became counterproductive to the free ministry of Jesus flowing among them? No system exists that cannot be exploited by those who will use it for their own gain, and often it's the leaders as much as those they hope to help.

What if instead of creating a widow's fund that needed administration, they would have asked the bigger question: Why are we neglecting to care for the neediest among us? Yes, that's more challenging. Yes, that means people have to look inside themselves and find a connection with Jesus that demonstrates itself in care for others. So they took the easy way out, and instead of challenging people to greater transformation and trust they created a program that made the problem someone else's responsibility.

The New Testament presents a great contrast between God's activity and our own. On the one hand, God does extraordinary things to invite people out of a broken world into the life of a new creation. On the other hand, flawed human attempts to organize that grace into viable systems distort the life of the church and beckon them back to the old creation of human effort. It didn't take long for the Galatians to abandon a gospel of grace and relationship for a system of religious performance. Believers in Corinth selfishly exploited one another and had already divided into factions and demonstrated that they were no longer living in the unity Jesus gives. In other places the young communities succumbed to sexual immorality and false teaching.

Even the solutions they came up with to resolve the problems often presented new ones. In Ephesus, Paul warned the elders that soon some would draw away people after their own desires. Later on he told Timothy to appoint elders in Ephesus to right the false doctrine being spread by would-be leaders. But that would only work as long as those elders were in fact listening to Jesus. By the time John writes to Ephesus, the elders had become the problem. One of them had set himself up as the senior pastor, lording over everyone else. So John had to alert them not to rely on the elders for truth, but to trust the Spirit within them.

And when Jesus addressed the Ephesian church in the book of Revelation they are lauded for their discernment between true and false teachers, but warned that it had come at the expense of their first love. If they did not return to that, they would no longer represent Jesus' church. In fact, of the seven churches John writes to in Revelation, only two of them are commended; the rest had given in to corruption and arrogance. In the two thousand years since, we continue to see these same themes. Like the early believers, we are so easily drawn back into the self-protecting mechanisms of the old creation rather than continuing to trust Jesus to build his church. Now we have two thousand years of Christian history to demonstrate that for the most part we haven't done any better.

Even a cursory look at the history of Christian institutions shows how days of renewal harden into movements that have replaced the priorities of the kingdom with the needs of an institution. When anyone dared to speak of reforming the status quo, they were rebuffed and either executed or forced out. Would-be reformers who were excommunicated soon began their own institutions that became as rigid as the ones they fled. At first that happened only rarely, but now the "church splits" are common. New congregations begin whenever a pastor-preneur wants to start one, and new denominations form when one congregation is popular enough that others want to franchise its name and program. We have created thousands of systems that we identify as the church and all of them have come up woefully short.

I can conclude that, but in the same breath agree that much good has been done through such institutions around the world in the name of Christ. Countless people have been comforted and helped by the Gospel message and our institutions have donated vast amounts of time and money to alleviate suffering all over the world with medical help, hunger relief, education, and other acts of compassion. For the most part Christian teaching has been clarified and numerous individuals have added to a rich heritage of literature. This still encourages people to know God and walk with him.

God still makes himself known through these efforts and many first meet him there. Most amazingly, the Gospel remains intact even if we believe it is "by grace and through faith" only for the first twenty-four hours, before we begin to instruct people of everything they need to do to be good Christians. Like the early followers the church seems most powerful at its most primitive, when our confidence in God is high and we haven't yet built systems to protect her.

Once built, however, our systems have proved more adept at wielding power in a worldly way than they are at shaping a community of the loved. So it's no surprise that our systems reflect the same priorities of earthly systems rather than those of Jesus. How did the opulence of the emperors of Rome differ at all from the opulence of the Roman Church? How did their temples differ from Christian cathedrals? Not at all! Even the pillars in many of the holy buildings of Rome were cannibalized from the Roman Forum itself.

The longer human institutions survive, the more privileged the ruling class becomes, the more excessive its buildings, and the more power can be manipulated to reward those who kneel at its altar. When what claims to be the church reflects the same values and utilizes the same methodologies of its culture, you can be sure something is amiss. You should see the luxurious green-rooms some mega-churches provide just behind the stage for their staff and guest speakers. It's no wonder the powers of Christianity have been on the wrong side of historical movements. They were so entrenched with royalty and dependent on authority that they couldn't support the growth of democratic movements until those movements prevailed. They resisted attempts to ennoble and protect women even though Jesus had treated them with dignity and equality. They were part of the power structure that used mission work as an excuse to conquer, plunder, and enslave indigenous people around the world.

Voices from a variety of quarters have been warning us for generations. Eberhard Arnold, a German theologian and founder of the Bruderhof, wrote in the early 1900s:

> Isn't the great world organization which names itself after Christ serving a god other than the God whom Jesus confessed, the God of a totally different order? Hasn't the institutional church sided with wealth and protected it, sanctified mammon, christened warships, and blessed soldiers going to war? Isn't the Christian state the most ungodly institution that ever existed? Aren't the state and the organized church, which protect privilege and wealth, diametrically opposed to the coming order of God?

In his penetrating book, *The Misunderstanding of the Church,* first published in 1952, Swiss theologian Emil Brunner documented the transition of the early church from a communion of persons united in Jesus, to members of a legal, administrative institution that emptied the church of its life and power. By displacing the real presence of Jesus for the celebration of sacraments, the church was "transformed from a spiritual *koinonia*, a unity of persons into a unity flowing from a common relationship to a thing, that is, a collective."

When Dr. John Sentamu, Archbishop of York, was installed in 2005, he quoted from Michael Ramsey who said in the 1960s,

"Why have we in England turned this glorious gospel of life in the Spirit into a cumbersome organization that repels, and whose people are dull and complacent?"

Why, indeed! Our institutions have created the same environment Jesus found among the scribes and Pharisees. An honest look at his words of warning to them in Matthew 23 exposes that we are guilty of the same practices that distort God's ways. Many preach a reality they don't live. They burden others down with the load of legalism while they live to excess. They posture to be seen as "building their platform" and compete for places of honor at banquets and meetings. Jesus told them not to use titles to exalt themselves above others, and we do it every day with pastors, bishops, doctorates, and elders. They talk of a kingdom they won't enter, and actually prevent others from doing so as well because of all their obligations. This Scripture is perhaps the one we ignore most. We violate it without concern or regret and by doing so have traded a vibrant life in Christ for an empty religion called Christianity. While it speaks of things that are true, in the end it doesn't offer people a way to live inside those truths with freedom.

For the most part, our steps down the dark road of institutionalism are made with the best of intentions. Seeking efficient ways to organize a group or protect it from false teaching, we define a set of expectations. Enforcing those expectations dehumanizes not only those whom they seek to control, but also those who think they lead. Few set out to create abusive systems, but few have the will to stop them when they no longer serve Jesus' purpose. What begins as simple structures to celebrate his life together, coalesce into institutions that perpetuate the ambitions of its leaders. Instead of teaching people to follow Jesus, they instruct people to follow his teachings as they have interpreted them and the rituals they have identified as essential. They even co-op the term *faith* as another word for their religion, instead of a growing trust in who God is.

Never has the gap been wider between what it means to be a good Christian and what it means to live in the life of Christ than it is in our day. Christianity has simply co-opted New Testament terminology to paint over old covenant realities. We are still preoccupied with law, priesthood, offerings, holy days, and sacred spaces. We even use *grace* in the name of congregations that are laced with vitriol and legalism. What Scriptures express as realities we've reduced to icons. Worship becomes a song service instead of living at the Father's pleasure. Fellowship is attending a congregational meeting instead of real friendships with other followers. Teaching is a lecture on Sunday morning, instead of illuminating the next step in someone's journey. Authority is derived from a position in an institution instead of speaking God's heart accurately. One can be a good Christian by fitting into a set of expectations and still not know Jesus or the transforming power he gives.

In the end, Christian history may not prove to be all that different from Israel's in the Old Testament—brief seasons of God's visitation followed by generations of unfaithfulness to him. As institutions age they tend to harden into intransigent systems and displace the simplicity of life in Christ for their own needs. Our two-thousand-year-old experiment proves that whenever we convey the life of the Spirit to an institutional arrangement, the institution wins—not always quickly, but eventually. While I'm grateful for the good they have accomplished they don't seem to be able to sustain a community of love nor display an accurate reflection of God's character.

How many congregations, mission groups, and Bible studies began as a small group of people in a home burned out on the rigidity of their previous group, hopeful for a better reflection of his life and love? Soon they grow into the very organization they had fled with the hope that this time all will go well because they have better people in charge. What they don't realize is that organizational needs shape its leaders, not the other way around.

Many start out well intentioned, hoping to reform the institution and bring it back in line with the priorities of Jesus. That effort is usually short-lived as the needs of the institution to protect the influence and resources of the group require greater control in the hands of fewer people. The simplicity of loving one another will eventually get swallowed up in the process no matter how hard we try to resist. In the end, our institutions end up just like everyone else's.

During my first trip to Israel, I was a little put off by some of the people on our pastor's tour who were trying to convert our Jewish guide, Abraham. They kept making snide asides to him as to why he wouldn't accept Jesus as the Messiah.

On the last day we stood by the bus as we were waiting for others to bring their bags from the hotel. I asked him if he had been offended by some of the things said to him on this trip.

He passed it off with a wave. "Not at all," he answered. "I've been doing this for twenty years. Everyone tries to convert me to their religion—Catholics, Pentecostals, Baptists, Reformed Jews, Orthodox Jews, Mormons, Muslims—everyone." Then he looked up at me with a smile. "Would you like to know why none of them convince me?"

"I would!" I replied.

"Come with me," he said as he led me around the front of the bus and onto the edge of the road. "Do you see that building down there with the Star of David on it?"

"Yes."

"That's ours."

"Do you see that steeple with the cross on it across the way?"

I nodded.

"That's yours."

And then he pointed me toward the dome of a mosque on a hillside not far away.

I nodded.

"That's theirs."

I smiled trying to imagine what he'd say next.

"Take off the Star of David, the cross, and the dome, and underneath aren't they really all the same thing? You would think if one of us were serving the Living God, it would look different."

He was right. Christianity doesn't look any different from the outside. It doesn't surprise me that all man-made religions have the same components at their core. The shame of the fall draws us into religious activity that seeks to appease an angry deity and to earn his favor by pleasing his expectations. That's why they are laced with fear, enamored with their sacred buildings, and led by local, holy-man gurus who officiate at rituals that at some times are meant to comfort the faithful, and at other times to threaten them for not working hard enough.

The fact is we don't look much different from other religious institutions, and we aren't even that different from other business enterprises. Wouldn't a community of people living in a vibrant relationship with Jesus do just about everything differently?

That it would!

6 | The Undeniable Longing

Where the Spirit of the Lord is, there is freedom.

2 CORINTHIANS 3:17

W hy are so many concluding that the congregation they have been part of for years may be doing more to distract them from following Jesus than encouraging them to do so?

They used to love it. It's where they first learned about God and his kingdom and enjoyed the camaraderie of life and fellowship. They were devoted participants, then active volunteers, and many became leaders because they wanted to help it fulfill its mission. Their vested interest was not in questioning the system, but in making it successful.

But something changed. Some can point to specific decisions or encounters with leadership that soured the relationship by pushing them in a direction they couldn't wholeheartedly support. Others report a growing recognition that the system they were in was at odds with a growing hunger to follow Jesus as he was making himself known to them. Friendships grew more superficial, lost to increased activity. Most assume this growing disillusionment is only spawned by bad experiences. But that wasn't true for me. I had some great experiences, opportunities, and friendships in the congregations I was part of that indelibly shaped my life.

But as good as they were they were always interrupted by our preoccupation with the program, and seasons of renewal would easily fade into drudgery.

For most of my life I vacillated between brief seasons of insight and passion for a deeper relationship with him and long stretches of frustration trying to fulfill that passion with the religious tools I'd been given. They were supposed to work. Everyone said so. How can you fault studying the Bible, praying, trying to be righteous, being active in a local fellowship, and learning from the teachings of others? I soaked up knowledge like one of those quilted paper towels and discovered that I had a gift to pass on to others what I had learned as well. But intellectual knowledge and ritualistic activities didn't help me find the freedom I hoped it would, nor did it promote the kind of relationships in which church life could thrive.

It's got to be better than this. The thought appears unbidden in your quieter moments and at first you're not even sure where it comes from. It could be a deeper longing left unfulfilled by your religious activity, something you read in Scripture that whetted your appetite, or struggling with yet another personal failure. Maybe it was a tinge of condemnation added to the sermon by a frustrated pastor, or feeling alone in a congregation full of people.

Frustration at the disparity between your hungers and your experience is a telltale sign of the new creation awakening in you. Express it, however, and you'll find others will discourage you from giving it too much weight, fearful that it will disturb the status quo or lead you into error. But the truth is they, too, have had the same thought before—many times! Not knowing what to do with it and having been discouraged by others themselves, they learned to suppress it and settle for what seemed to satisfy so many others. After all, who are you to challenge two thousand years of religious development? If there were something better, others would have found it by now. With a little self-talk, the rogue thought can easily be dismissed, but only for a while.

Months later in another situation the thought emerges again like a pesky mosquito buzzing around your ear at night. And while it may feel like harassment if you don't know what to do with it, it is actually a gift. It's the new creation finding its way to the surface. You're beginning to see through the limitations of man's effort and hungering for something more real than the artificial activity religious structures offer. As I've watched people go through this process in the last twenty years, it seems that deeper longing continues to surface in two expressions: *There must be something more* or *Something seems wrong here.*

Sometimes that was a very generalized feeling and at other times a specific response to a situation. I knew what the Scripture said church could be, and I had tasted of her on enough occasions in my youth to know she was real. I hungered for people to have that experience and knew that our activities were not promoting it, even though we tried. I didn't realize at the time that since our methods were conformity-based we were unwittingly subverting the very open, transformative relationships we were wanting people to have.

I also had moments with a foreboding sense that what I was doing flew in the face of things Jesus had said. I can't tell you how many times Luke 14 came to mind as I sought more influence in my younger days. Jesus told his disciples not to push for the places of honor, but to take the back seat and let God move them into the place he had for them. But the people I saw advancing were given to self-promotion and personal branding. When I tried it, however, this passage would spring to mind and I was forced to choose between trusting him to put me where he wanted or join the melee of people fighting to be king of the hill.

Another Scripture that surfaced often was Jesus' words about leadership. He told his disciples that they were not going to exercise authority over people the way the world did it, but like him find their fruitfulness in serving others. We called our approach "servant leadership," not realizing how oxymoronic the term was to our application. We drew the pyramids upside down, but it was clear who exercised authority to make the system work.

When that longing surfaces either as a hunger for something more real, or as a restlessness that something is wrong, it presents us with a critical moment of choice. Do I stick to the comfort of what I've always known or take the risk to follow my heart into a more undefined place? Unfortunately most people will encourage you to suppress your hunger. I've talked to hundreds of church leaders who have had similar moments of being pulled between what Scripture invited them to and what they have to do to keep their institutional position. Many have told me they would love to embrace a different reality but can't figure out how to make it work. With sad and heavy eyes, they've turned to me, "I've decided just to make the best of what I already have."

I did that, too, for way too many years, settling into a comfortable, though often lifeless, regimen and ignoring the deeper call of my heart. There were always enough breadcrumbs in the routine to give me enough hope that if we could just find the right alignment all would be well. For a long time I thought it was my fault, knowing how lazy I could be as well as the temptations and motivations that rumbled just beneath the surface. I kept trying harder to be a better person. As genuine as that may seem it always proved a side road back into the swamp of failed self-effort and frustration.

When I was on staff I blamed the leadership above me for sticking to routines that had become lifeless. When I was a pastor I blamed the congregation for not risking enough. When I pressed for changes I thought would revive us, I was surprised that others didn't share my passion. When I was able to implement some new idea, it always fell short of the outcome I'd hoped for. I share the frustration of one pastor in Sacramento, who expressed it this way: "I've tried seeker-sensitive, purpose-driven, cell church, house church, organic church all to no avail. What do I try now?" Only after numerous failed attempts do we even consider that our human systems may be part of the problem.

As our hunger grows for the reality of the new creation, so does our frustration with the old. While it does offer moments of initial excitement, it always ends in futility. Try as we might to work our ideas, they will never produce the joy of the new creation we so desperately seek. That's why after trying multiple congregations, implementing a new program, or even trying new ways of doing "church," we end up back in the same place. The life of God that we seek seems like a mirage on the horizon, and just when we think we're getting close, it vanishes and a new apparition appears even farther away.

If we let our hunger grow, however, we will begin to see through the emptiness and futility of our own labors and that something more will appear. It's expressed well in this email I got in response to a podcast I host at The God Journey for people thinking outside the box of organized religion. Speaking of me and my co-host, he wrote:

> Why do I listen to these guys? I have never met them, they often say things that sound heretical, use strange terminology, seem lazy and disorganized at times, and yet I look forward to their humor, their snarky remarks, and the challenging way they view Scripture. Me, on the other hand, find myself at 53, tired, angry, and bitter about many things in my last twenty-six years as a pastor. I am in a situation many of my peers would die for—stable, bills are paid, supportive leadership team, people wanting to spend time with me, etc. All I know at this point is that I need to deal with my heart. I don't want to spend the next 20 years or more of productive ministry the way I have spent the last 26. So, from Mr. D. Min, church planter, pastor, I say keep up the good work.

That's the new creation awakening in him, and though he's not sure where it will lead, he's at the threshold of a different journey. He will soon discover that the new creation is not out on the horizon somewhere; it is already within him. Jesus is inviting him to follow him instead of attempting to meet the expectations of others. Without that growing sense of futility in the old creation, none of us would ever look beyond what we can do on our own. Losing confidence in our human effort is a big step on this journey.

So instead of dying in the frustration of failed human effort, we can pursue the "something more" that the new creation invites us into. A friend of mine expressed this reality when describing his engagement with people who stimulate his spiritual journey. "When I am with them life is more. There is *more* laughing, more playing, more eating, more heart-felt conversations, more sensing the presence and purposes of God, in short, *more real living!*"

That's the "something more" I was looking for too. It wasn't perfect people but real people on a transforming journey. When I'm with like people, I am more aware of God and my conversations are more honest and more filled with love and generosity. I laugh more in sheer delight, cry more when touched by people's pain, and come away encouraged and wiser. In the new creation no one has to pretend to be better than they are and people's weaknesses only make them more endearing.

That's the fruit of lives growing to know him, not the result of creating a group and trying to get people to conform to its expectations and obligations. That's what I'd been trying to do for twenty years and no wonder I kept falling short. The way to share this kind of life together is to connect with people who are awakening in the new creation as well, so don't look for another system to follow.

You cannot find it in a book, including this one. The new creation is that space in our hearts where we know that we are deeply loved by God and where we have a growing awareness of how he thinks and invites us to live in the world. It is not guidelines to follow, but insight inside our circumstances—the law of God written in the heart. Jesus didn't teach his disciples a new code to live by; he taught them how to live alongside his Father without the guilt and fear that drive our religious systems.

When you begin to question two thousand years of tradition,

you can expect others to be threatened and try to discourage you. They will misinterpret your frustration as bitterness and accuse you of being selfish. They will discount your hungers by saying that we can't expect the church to be perfect when it is filled with broken humanity. They will tell you that we can't just sit around and do nothing when there is so much work to be done. Most of all they will be afraid that in leaving long-established traditions you risk your own salvation. Following him even when others wrongly judge and exclude you is why so few take this road. Those who do only do so because they are convinced that there is a reality beyond their experience that continues to beckon them.

Jack was a surgeon missionary from Scotland to the Congo in the 1950s and had to leave during the revolution. He ended up in New Zealand working as a surgeon and eventually as a hospital administrator. During that time he was deeply involved in congregational activities, including serving on elder boards and other committees. One day twenty-five years ago, as he was praying about his ongoing frustration about the state of the church, a thought came across his mind that he attributed to Jesus: "If you want to be part of the church I'm building, you have to leave the one man is building."

So he resigned his positions in the congregation and found himself on an extraordinary journey that many others have taken. Do I think we all have to leave our congregations to see the one Jesus is building? If you are already part of a generous faith community that isn't performance-based, you may be able to embrace that life without leaving. Others have found it necessary to leave because the dynamics are so destructive. What we can all do is stop thinking that the church humanity is building and the one church Jesus is building are the same thing. Sometimes they overlap, but they are not the same, and if we don't know that we will continue to get lost in our human efforts to replicate what cannot be achieved by human effort.

What we need is not a better system to manage but a different kind of person who is learning to live in a new creation.

7 | A New Kind of Person

If anyone is in Christ, he is a new creation;
the old has gone, the new has come!

2 CORINTHIANS 5:17

Six months after I left the pastorate, I was invited by some people in Australia to teach at a camp. While they had been deeply touched by my first book, *The Naked Church*, they also knew its message was incomplete. Though it explained the failure of our religious systems to put intimacy with God at the core of their mission, and while it painted a hopeful picture of what life in Christ could be, it still relied on reforming that system to a better end. As we were discussing how the book impacted them one afternoon, one of the camp organizers gently said, "As much as we love the book we know that you have not yet realized that Jesus did not leave us with a system to manage, but his Spirit to follow."

The words jarred me. Though they rang with truth they also seemed dangerous and perhaps better left unexplored. I had a two-inch-thick file at home with my notes about "A New Structure" for the "church" that I had been crafting during the previous years and would be, or so I hoped, the material for a new book. The idea that it would just offer up another human attempt to devise a structure to add to all the other structures we've tried during two thousand years, made me sick to my stomach.

But that's what we've always done, haven't we? When our structures fail us, someone devises yet another one for us to try. My shelves are filled with books offering a variety of fixes to cure what ails the church. None of them work, which is why new ones are published every year. What if the church of Jesus Christ isn't built on human systems at all, but with "living stones" (I Peter 2:15)—those people who are learning to live by the breath of the Spirit instead of human ingenuity?

It would take me years to unpack what I heard that day and find the adventure they encouraged me to embrace. Jesus invited us into a relationship with his Father that would allow his Spirit to rewrite our lives from the inside out. Our engagements with him would alter our affections, expose and heal our coping mechanisms, and untwist the bondage of our self-preferring lives. Instead of encouraging people to embrace that journey, we take the easier, though completely ineffective route of creating systems we think will produce those outcomes.

So we search the Scriptures to craft a set of principles we think will make us good Christians and then try to live up to them. We turn the fruits of the Spirit, for example, into a list of obligations. Be more loving, more patient, kinder, and gentler. We will try, of course, but in time the list becomes less an encouragement and more the source of condemnation whenever we fall short of our own expectations.

No one told us about the new creation already inside us, or how to embrace it. We were simply told to pray, read their Bibles, live by God's rules, and love others as best we could. And above all, attend "church" and submit to the traditions and doctrines that have stood for centuries. Initially it is all new and exciting. The lights, music, and sermons offer insights that help illuminate God and encourage us to live a better life.

It doesn't take long, however, to realize that we can't live up to all the expectations placed on us. We may live better for a while but we can't sustain it, and many grow discouraged thinking they are the only ones who can't make it work. That's where I was for a time. I found I couldn't change myself, at least in the ways that mattered. Oh, I could act differently for months at a time but old temptations would return in seasons of despair or frustration. I just learned to hide them better. When I became a professional Christian by going "into the ministry" fresh out of college, I found it was easier to keep the rules so that others would see me as more spiritual. While I found it easy to avoid those sins we consider more egregious, mine merely morphed into the same religious arrogance the Pharisees displayed by holding in contempt those who did not work as hard as I did. All of this was done with the best of intentions and a plethora of ignorance. In my mind I was trying to be better for God. I thought I was overcoming sin when I was only repressing it, and I thought I was helping others by pressuring them to do what I thought was best for them.

I was caught between two worlds—the self-effort of performance-based religion and the new creation growing inside of me. I didn't know it at the time, but the two are incompatible. On the day we are regenerated in Christ we enter a new form of existence: "If anyone is in Christ, he is a new creation; the old has gone, the new has come!" (2 Corinthians 5:17) That Scripture has perplexed many because even after they connected with Jesus they didn't feel like a new creation. Sure, they may have been overjoyed with the forgiveness and new sense of love that flooded their hearts, but they soon discovered that they fell prey to the same temptations, doubts, and selfishness they knew before. They conclude Paul was either talking about an abstract truth or they relegate its fulfillment to eternity.

But Paul was talking in concrete terms. We actually become a new creation ready to live in a new reality. Unfortunately we reduced Christianity to a religion by pulling the teachings of Jesus into the old creation and trying to apply them in systems that depend on human effort. The old creation is deeply rooted in human selfishness and even our religious attempts must appeal to self-interest either with threats of punishment or promises of blessing.

In the animated film *Finding Nemo*, the seagulls constantly cried, "Mine! Mine! Mine!" as they picked at one another and fought over every morsel they could find. There's perhaps no better image to reflect the nagging disposition of our flesh that seeks to be served by maximizing whatever joy might be ours or by minimizing whatever pain may come our way. This self-preferring nature of our flesh makes us relationally challenged and lies behind every human system designed to manage our conflicts.

Evidence of the old creation can always be found in its preoccupation with cash, credit, and control as a way to satisfy the flesh. The love of money, comfort, and possessions, our thirst for other people's approval and applause, and our desire to get our way over others overlay almost every human interaction from personal relationships to the systems we design to advance our cause. They disproportionately reward a few people at the top while exploiting everyone else to keep it running. Those at the top seem incapable of resisting the corruption and indulgence that comes with excess, celebrity, and power. One only has to look at Washington, DC, Wall Street, or Hollywood to see how cash, credit, and control warp our culture and destroy the lives of those who seek them. Some of this is obviously formal and far reaching, but it is no less destructive when someone uses the homeowner's association as their own fiefdom, exploits a friend with shame, or manipulates their spouse with a cold shoulder.

Even our Christian institutions are dominated by these concerns, which demonstrate just how much they reflect the old creation instead of the new. The best religion can offer is to broker those competing demands by managing money, offering validation, and manipulating others to do its bidding. When

I was a pastor I spent the bulk of my time not helping hungry people grow, but managing the political realities of people seeking these very things. The pressing needs were never about spiritual growth, but about the tangled web of money, approval, and power. Scripture warns us how they blind us, and history demonstrates how often we create structures that end up rewarding those ambitions and exploiting the powerless.

People who don't know Jesus and how he works have an insatiable desire for money, acclaim, and power. Conflict ensues as people maneuver to get what they want; when they do it in God's name they will justify any tactic. I was part of a team that helped write and then release what became an international best-selling book. The three years in which we wrote that book together and then distributed it out of a garage in Southern California was one of the most spiritually engaging, intellectually stimulating, and personally rewarding experiences of my life. The generosity and friendship that grew as we wrestled through a thousand decisions was palpable. As we shared that story with others, many were undone with their desire to be inside relationships of mutual caring and respect, instead of the ones they were used to that are filled with competition and conflict. We all knew what we had participated in was way beyond what any of us could have accomplished alone. We came to appreciate in a fresh way that God himself is a community, and we saw that his desire in creation was to invite us into that collaborative. We saw firsthand what incredible things can happen when people share their gifts freely.

We promised each other that we would value the relationship more than the rewards. We even wrote about how humanity always resorts to systems to manage conflict, instead of sorting them out in the honesty and compassion of relationship. Initially our agreements were all verbal and we joked how tenuous that was if any of us fell back to the old creation's preoccupation with cash, credit, and control. I was hopeful, but I'd been in similar circumstances where people will promise the moon when it benefits them and change drastically when they have to follow through on their promises.

But I believe in the power of collaboration when it rises out of unity, honesty, and generosity. Nothing is more thrilling when it works and few things more painful when it comes unraveled. I told the team early on that I never again wanted to be part of brothers turning on each other. I promised them if conflict ever surfaced I would make sure they walked away with a smile on their face before I did. No one thought we would need it.

And then it all went wrong. As book sales grew, family, friends, agents, managers, and lawyers came out of the woodwork to claim a stake in the project. For some it was no longer a gift, but a cash cow to be milked. Whispered rumors and backroom agreements began to subvert open and honest friendship. Demands and ultimatums replaced dialog; friendships were trampled underfoot. Even though every decision we had made for three years had been unanimous, eventually one filed a lawsuit in an attempt to assume control of what we'd done together. The language shifted from the generosity of collaboration to the need for control.

My heart broke. Appeals for reconciliation, mediation, and even a conversation were rebuffed in favor of legal proceedings. Unfortunately it only takes one person and one moment to destroy years of relationship. Why anyone would trade the joy of friendship for cheap trinkets is beyond me, but it happens often. Once people start claiming what they think they deserve instead of sharing freely the wonder of God's gifts, we slide out of the new creation and back into the old. The book we wrote remains a great story. It has touched lives the world over and continues to do so, but the story behind it is now less a reflection of the way God works. I am still hopeful the last chapter of that story has yet to be written.

Jesus invited us into something so much more profound and transforming than our continued preoccupation with cash, credit, and control and the chaos that results from fighting over them. The life of the church is not found in managing these concerns in institutions, but in the liberation of people from the very appetites that make us competitors instead of collaborators. Hope for the church is not in some as yet undiscovered system, but in a different kind of person who lives at the pleasure of Jesus instead of seeking his own.

Jesus demonstrated his freedom from these preoccupations in the temptations of the wilderness. He refused to use miracles on a whim even for his provision, to employ a cheap stunt to wow the crowds, or to grasp power to command the world. John told us these are not from God's realm but from our broken human world. "For everything in the world—the cravings of sinful man, the lust of his eyes and the boasting of what he has and does— comes not from the Father but from the world." (1 John 2:16)

Can you imagine the kind of community that would be unleashed on the world if the people in it were more preoccupied with the realities of Jesus' kingdom—faith, hope, and love—than they were with their own provision, significance, and power? It would be amazing but it is not something human effort can produce. Our response to the appetites of the flesh and our passion for his kingdom are more visceral. Healing does not come by knowing better and trying harder. That only works for a short season. We cannot divorce ourselves from the world of money or the manipulations of power because it is part of the elementary principles of this age. We can, however, negotiate them without letting them own us or using them to exploit others.

That's what he wants to do in you and it will happen as you grow more confident in his love and more aware of his purpose in things that surround you. The appetites of the flesh are crowded out as we are won into a better kingdom that has far more value than the things we use to fill our empty souls. As he becomes more real the priorities of the world really do fade away. What seemed so important without him, suddenly seem meaningless with him.

Lives that are being transformed are the seedbed out of which Jesus' church takes expression. Notice that's a continuing action, not an accomplished product. It doesn't require perfect people, just those on a journey of being shaped by Jesus. Those engaged in that process are far more relational than those who try to manage each other's foibles. Those who live inside the old creation can't help but see their success in needing to convince others they are right, having to be in charge, and being the center of attention. They will push for their own interests even when they have to exploit others to do so. It turns every connection into a contest of wills and can only be brokered by clear lines of decision-making authority.

Those growing in a relationship with Jesus, however, don't share the same angst. They realize the structures of this world cannot accomplish the work of the kingdom and that Jesus' reality supersedes the things that are valued in this age. Trusting God for their resource, they don't have to manipulate people for money. Resting in God's acceptance of their lives, they don't look for their validation by what others think or say. And, knowing that Jesus gets the last word on everything, they see no need to claim power over others.

The old creation makes us relationally challenged, which is why meetings that include such people have to be heavily managed. What do you do with the know-it-all theologian who loves to hear herself talk, the broken person who draws attention to himself, the selfish and dishonest who use the group for their own needs, or the woman with a ministry that wants to take the group captive to her gift?

Living in the new creation changes everything about the way people relate to one another, and the result is they don't have to be managed. They are gracious in conflict, quick to seek forgiveness, and quick to offer it. They don't carry agendas to push on others, and they look out for the interests of others as well as their own. They see themselves as part of a larger kingdom that is not in their control and they freely embrace what Jesus asks of them. They are a joy to be with and people come away from them encouraged and stimulated in their own journey. This is a different kind of person who gives expression to the church, and that's why the passion they have for those still trapped in the old creation is not to control them, but to love them into a different reality that will free them from their self-preferring coping mechanisms that destroy their relationships with others.

Participating in the new creation is an invitation to all, but never a demand. You can live in the old if you want. God will still love you and make himself known to you, but his desire will be to win you into his love so that you can enter the more spacious place your heart desires.

8 | Won Into Love

This is love: not that we loved God, but that he loved us...

1 JOHN 4:10

There's only one thing I want to convey in this chapter, and if you already know it, you're welcome to move on to the next. But be careful, most people who think they know it only know it intellectually, and that's where it counts least. What is it? The God of the universe loves you more than anyone on this planet ever has or ever will.

I know. I thought I knew it, too. You can't be a Christian long and not be comfortable with the verbiage. Nothing is more theologically certain than that God loves. Our favorite Scriptures talk about it and so do our songs. It's Theology 101, after all. The Old Testament, even with its scary stories of God's judgment, also overflows with God's love. More than three hundred verses talk about God's compassion. Repeatedly it declares that "the Lord is slow to anger, abounding in love," that his love is better than life, that it endures forever, and that we can trust in his unfailing love. Even the most pain-filled book, Lamentations, declares that "his mercies are new every morning."

In the New Testament, love is the predominant theme and John wrote that it is the very essence of God himself—"God is love." (I John 4:8) Love isn't his possession, nor does he give it as a gift. He is love itself. It defines his nature and allows Father, Son, and Spirit to share life together as they trust, commune, and cooperate in perfect harmony.

As important as it is to appreciate his love intellectually, that alone didn't comfort me in trouble, set me at ease in failure, or draw me to him as the most endearing presence in the universe. I grew up with conflicting images of God, as loving Father, surely, but also as a terrifying and angry judge. How he felt about me on any given day depended on how good I could be. When I did what pleased him, then he would love me. When I struggled or failed, however, I wanted him a million miles away. My theology of God's love had been twisted into something I had to earn, which allowed me to talk about it as a concept while negating it in the same breath.

I know I'm not alone. I can't tell you how many times people have told me that someone gave them a copy of my book *He Loves Me*, and they put it on their shelf thinking, *Who doesn't know that?* Months or years later they finally picked it up and discovered that there is a world of difference between assenting to the principle that God loves them and living every day as his beloved child. Many find it easier to believe God is either disappointed in them or too distant to make a difference in the brutalities of life. They don't yet know that God holds more delight for them than I have for my children or grandchildren, and that's saying something.

I was not prepared for how deeply I would love my grand-daughter on the night she was born. As excited as I was about having a grandchild, I honestly didn't know how I would love her as much as I loved my own children. The hours leading up to her birth were excruciating for my daughter as she suffered through thirty-two hours of intense, posterior labor, and I thirty-two hours of anguish thinking of what she was going through. Eventually, her doctor wanted to do a Caesarean delivery but my daughter begged for one more chance to have her naturally. That time it worked. When I heard the news all I could think about was how much I wanted to hold my daughter and tell her how proud I was of her. I was not prepared for what happened when I saw that little bundle lying on my daughter's chest. My heart soared with affection for someone I didn't yet know. It was not something I contemplated or conjured. In an instant my affection for her was immediate and deep, although she had not done one thing to trigger it.

Does God teem with similar affection for you? I'm sure of it, though in a far deeper way than our human emotions can reflect. What's more, Jesus made a way for us to know that love tangibly. You don't have to take someone's word for it and try to convince yourself to believe it. It's a revelation in the heart that comes from knowing him and seeing how he responds to us.

This is his to win, not ours to find. I have been winning my granddaughter into my love for nine years now. I didn't expect her to figure it out on her own or to trust me because I told her so. I convince her by how I treat her. It may be God's greatest joy to win people into his affection, no less for you than a woman at a well, a greedy tax collector in a tree, or a terrified fisherman who had betrayed him. Love reaches out to the beloved and seeks to win them into a relationship. That's what courtship is about and hopefully marriage, too. Every day presents more opportunity to win a heart, even if it takes a lifetime.

One of the best letters I ever received came from a man whose dad had been a pastor in a brutal, legalistic denomination. As he was dying of cancer, he was stricken with fear that he hadn't done enough to earn his salvation. His son, who had long before rejected his father's legalism, read him each night from my book about God's love. I began to weep just reading the opening of his letter to me: "My dad came to the awareness of his Father's love one hour before he passed away last night...."

Jesus' purpose was not to make us worthy of God's love, but to set us free to see that we already have it. And yet so many have missed this detail. A few years ago I was asked to participate in a study of Godly love as a new academic discipline, and two researchers were sent to record an interview with me as part of their research. As they set up the video equipment in my living room they asked if I had any questions for them.

I did. "What's this study based on?"

"It's based on the Great Command," one of them replied.

"And what is that?" I asked.

They both looked at each other a bit surprised then back at me. "You don't know the Great Command?"

Of course I did; I just wanted to see if they did since most are wrong on this question.

"It's to love God with all your heart and your neighbor as yourself," she continued.

"Oh, so this is an Old Testament study." I smiled hoping to get them thinking.

Now they looked even more stunned. "What do you mean? Jesus is the one who said it."

"That he did. But he was quoting from Deuteronomy in answer to what was the greatest command of the law. Didn't he later give his followers a new command?"

"A new command I give you: Love one another. As I have loved you...." (John 13:34–35) It seems to me that by giving a new command, Jesus superseded the previous one, and he did so in a way that strikes to the heart of the New Covenant itself. The old command began with us—our obedience to love God with everything we are and to love our neighbors as we love ourselves. Jesus began somewhere else, not with our ability to love, but with God's love toward us. Come to know that and you'll not only love him back but you'll also love well in the world. That alone, Jesus said, would convince the whole world that we are his.

John explained further in his epistle. "This is love: not that we loved God, but that he loved us and sent his Son as an atoning sacrifice for our sins." (I John 4:10) Love originates in him. Left to ourselves, we tend to define love in selfish terms. When someone is kind to us or gives us what we want, we feel loved. But when they cease to treat us the way we want, we question their love. Couples even talk about falling "out of love" when their needs are no longer served. Until we discover how loved we are by him, we have no hope of loving others. That's why John called it first love. How many times have you been beat over the head at a revival or a retreat for leaving your first love as if it is your responsibility to conjure up the feelings of love you had for God when you first came to know him? First love is not how much we love him, but how deeply God loves you. When we lose sight of his love all kinds of things—fear, insecurity, and anxiety—creep in and draw us back to the old creation.

I was taught that love wasn't a feeling but a commitment. We separated love from heartfelt affection, I assume, so we could pretend to love someone we didn't actually like. It was a fatal mistake, though, because we came to see God's love for us in the same way—as a commitment rather than real affection—and our love for him as a command that required us to pretend we loved him even if he seemed detached and unconcerned. We missed the deeper affection and delight he has for each of us, and though that transcends our emotions it does help shape them. Knowing how loved you are by God invites you into a river of affection that draws you into him as an endearing presence in the universe and also flows from you toward others.

"Jesus asked us to love our neighbor, right?" The man stood among a room full of eight hundred Kenyan pastors to ask me a question while I was sharing about Father's affection. "What if your neighbor raped your wife and burned down your house? Am I supposed to love him?" The gripping pain in his voice made it clear this was not a hypothetical question. Only three years before, this region had been devastated by tribal violence following a disputed election that resulted in the rape and murder of thousands.

It would have been the height of presumption for me to tell him that loving his enemy was something God required of him. When we see God's love as affection, how could he possibly conjure up such an attachment to someone who had so heinously attacked his family? Jesus telling us to love our enemies is the same as asking the disciples to feed five thousand with a little boy's lunch. Left to ourselves, it is an impossible task. Only he can give us love like that. When Jesus told us to love our enemies, he was actually letting us know that he has enough love to pour into our hearts that one day we will have affection even for those who have deeply wronged us.

But that is an amazing process that can take significant time. I imagine there are as many ways to win us into his affection as there are people in the world. It took him more than forty years in my case. Looking back, I now see how God was whispering his love into my heart since my earliest days, but the tentacles of religious performance continued to lure me away from that reality and every pain and disappointment incited my mistrust. If he loved me, how could he not heal me of a childhood disease that brought no end of embarrassment? If he loved me, how could he let my childhood friend die of a brain tumor at seventeen? If he loved me, how could he let a colleague betray me with lies and ruin my reputation with a group of people I loved? It's been twenty years since I've asked those questions, not because he answered them all but because he won me into a love so large it consumed any evidence I had to the contrary.

That revelation came clear in a walk through a plum orchard. Four years before in the exact same spot, I felt God asked me to give up my paycheck from the congregation I was in and let him provide for me as I continued to serve them. Almost as soon as the thought ran through my mind, I dismissed it as wishful thinking. In the two years that followed, my frustrations grew as I was hemmed in by people's expectations. Two years later, after the betrayal of trust by a close friend, I found myself outside of that group, without a salary or severance. Though I looked for other work initially, God asked me to keep doing what he asked of me and he would provide. And he did, often by extraordinary means. I refused to help him by making my need known to others. He continued to graciously care for us even as he walked me through the pain and resentment I felt every day. Six months into that process I heard a story of Jesus' death on the cross that satisfied the brokenness of humanity, not an angry God's demand for justice. (I cover that in *He Loves Me*, and also in an online audio series called *Transitions* at lifestream.org.) If it were true, God the Father was an endearing personality in the redemption story, not an offended and disappointed deity.

I was suspicious at first and came home to study every Scripture on the atonement to see what I could learn. Increasingly, I found myself won into a different story of God's redemption. That, coupled with God's continued provision and losing my need for other people's approval in the aftermath of our congregational implosion, the penny dropped, as they say. I was walking through the plum orchard in the exact same spot where God had asked me four years before to give up my salary. Though I had ignored him originally, when it was forced on me two years later, he became my provision. Recognizing his mercy in the face of my disobedience undid me.

I knew in that moment I was loved by an awesome Father, who was able to work in me beyond my weaknesses. I knew that if I never did one more thing for God he would not love me one bit less than he did in that moment. And, yet, it was the richness of that love that made me want to do whatever he would ask me to do. This is what Paul meant when he wrote "the love of Christ compels us." (2 Corinthians 5:14) The way he loves us is so compelling that we will follow him to the ends of the earth. It's a love that invites us into transformation at a level I never thought possible.

I've heard enough stories from others to know there is no way to standardize the creative work of Jesus in winning us into his Father's affection. For some people it is coming to the end of themselves in a cathartic moment of surrender. For others it's a growing conviction over time. For one woman it came while sitting at her computer after two years of depression over her daughter's suicide. She was going to kill herself that evening if she couldn't find one hopeful sign that God was real. Somehow she landed on just such an article that turned her world upside down. For another it came at the end of her stripper act one evening. Raised in a Christian home, she'd become pregnant at sixteen and had been forced to perform by her drug-dealing boyfriend. Backstage, she found a single, red rose and a note from three women who were in the club that night offering her God's love and their help if she ever wanted to leave the lifestyle.

If you don't yet know how deeply loved you are by God, I have no idea what it will take. All you can do is give Jesus enough space for him to show you. Anything that makes you feel disqualified from that—be it egregious sin, abuse in your past, or challenges in your present—is a lie. He loves us all, each of us in the whole world. He wants you to know that in your own heart, not just read it in a book. Discovering that is not something you achieve. Since it's already true for you, even if you don't know it, it is simply something that you can relax into. Ask him to show you and watch for his fingerprints as life unfolds around you.

Learn to hold lightly anything that argues against his love. We've all had unanswered prayers and wrestled with how could God love us and not intervene. Our expectation of what his love must compel him to do is deeply grounded in the brokenness of humanity and our desire for comfort and security in something other than him. God's love is tangible enough to consume our most ardent doubts and disappointments. He's been entreating you into that love since the day you were born. Just because you haven't recognized him yet doesn't mean he isn't doing all he can do to win you. Just keep on asking, seeking, and knocking. It may take some time. He's not withholding from you; he is untangling the thoughts you have that are unworthy of him and of yourself. The entire redemption story, as well as its crowning moment on the cross, screams the truth that nothing here and nothing in eternity can separate you from his affection. (Romans 8)

This may seem a diversion from our discussion about finding church, but I can assure you it is not. The church of Jesus Christ is the community of the loved. So many of our management techniques depend on manipulating people's need for significance: their insecurities, their shame, and their fears. That's why religious institutions give gold-foiled stars to Sunday school students and "gold brick" recognition to big-givers of the new facility as well as lace their sermons with guilt. When you know you're loved such things will not manipulate you, and neither will you use them to manipulate others.

A community of people so convinced of Father's affection that they are able to genuinely love, honor, and care for others is very different from a collection of people who still live by the dictates of the old creation. That's why discipleship precedes community. Every human dysfunction is the result of living as if we are not loved. When people begin to discover how loved they are then they will live increasingly in his new creation and the community it spawns.

9 | Loved Into Life

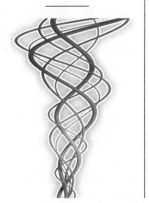

We have come to know and have believed
the love which God has for us.

I JOHN 4:16 (NASB)

For centuries our Christian systems have been preoccupied with getting people to abstain from sin and live as righteously as they can before God. In *Divine Conspiracy,* Dallas Willard called it the Gospel of Sin Management, which really is no Gospel at all. At the end of the day we're still focused on our sin, which only gives it more power. When Paul warned us that the mind set on the flesh is death and is unable to please God (Romans 8), he was not just talking about the mind set on indulging the flesh. He was also talking about the mind set on abstaining from it. Either way, the flesh is still the focus and we will fall victim to it.

When we hear of well-known Christians who are exposed for closeted failures, we assume they are hypocrites delighting in sin while they pretend to be righteous for the congregation or the cameras. The reality is far different. They've only learned to deal with their inner temptations by abstinence and accountability, hoping by sheer strength of will to keep their demons at bay. And it will work, for weeks or months at a time. Eventually, however, the energy runs out, and in moments of weakness or discouragement the temptation once again proves irresistible.

The problem with these systems is that no one gives you credit for the three months you avoided sin; they only blame you for the weakened moment you fell to it. Most of those who fall don't drive home reveling in the pleasure of their sin. Its pleasure was gone as soon as the temptation did its work. Most end up in a swamp of self-condemnation, promising God they will never, ever fail again. And they don't for months at a time, until the darker moment comes again and the cycle repeats.

Paul knew well the deception of performance-based righteousness. It cannot conquer sin. While it gives an appearance of righteousness, it lacks any value in actually restraining sensual indulgence. (Colossians 2:26) Whatever sinful behavior it mitigates on the outside only drives it into other places, such as religious arrogance, demanding others perform as well as we imagine we are. That's exactly how Paul became the chief of sinners (I Timothy 1:16) before his engagement with Jesus on a road to Damascus.

While performance is critical to navigate the old creation, it has no value in the new. In that sphere it is the gravity that draws us back from living in God's freedom and only leads us to guilt when we fail and arrogance when we succeed. That's why our religious accountability systems cannot produce real community. They exhaust us with an endless need to perform, compete, and pretend.

As God wins us into his love, however, a different kind of gravity takes over, much like our *Apollo* astronauts experienced in their flight as they reached the point when the gravitational pull of the moon had more effect on them than earth's gravity. At first the reality of his affection for us seems faint. Everything we know seems to argue against it. We may see hints of it here and there, like the moon's gravity playing on our tides, but it doesn't seem strong enough to overcome the draw of the world. As we continue to lean into him, however, we start to see his hand moving in our lives and get drawn into his purpose unfolding in us. Somewhere along the way, trusting his love becomes easier than doubting it and that's where we gain traction. No longer absorbed in our wants and needs, our perspective shifts to encompass what God is doing in us and in others around us, and that will allow us to live differently in the world.

It may be what John referred to when he said, "We know and rely on the love God has for us." (I John 4:16) Some translations draw out a deeper meaning: "We have come to know...," indicating a process. So often our confidence in his love is thwarted by our fears and doubts and circumstances we don't understand. I love the picture of an older John rejoicing that at last he had "come to know" and "come to rely" on the love God had for him.

I am continually amazed at the places my growing confidence in Father's love leads me. How great can it grow? I don't know, but I look forward to each day to discover what new freedom overtakes me and how that leads to treating others differently. Three words help me recognize God's gravity that replaces the pressures of the world: compassion, trust, and rest. As these emerge from our growing relationship with God, we'll find it easier to cooperate with God's working. They are the headwaters that allow us to join the flow of his church.

Compassion

Every "church group" talks about loving one another, but in most, especially the larger ones, people don't even know each other. Love is not an abstract commitment to the nameless; it's a genuine affection for people around us. I can be kind to anyone, patient with everyone, but having affection for someone is a deep delight in the heart. I may not like everything they do, but I am affected by their presence. I am interested in their well-being, and I am delighted to assist them however I am able, even if at great cost.

Dave originally came into my life while I was still a pastor. He used to pastor in a different denomination and we became good friends. After a few years, I noticed Dave and his wife no longer came to our services. We still connected outside of the congregation, but not as frequently. A couple of years later, they returned during the conflict that eventually led to my departure. After the collapse I asked Dave where they had been in the meantime.

"I'm sorry," he responded. "I knew you were about to get run over by those who loved power more than you did. I just couldn't bear to watch it happen."

"But then why did you come back for the worst of it?"

"That's the other thing," he answered, shaking his head. "I just couldn't let you go through it alone."

That's a great picture of Godly compassion—"to come to passion," in the Old English sense of rushing to suffering. If you love someone you'll want to be with him in pain, even when you feel inadequate and even if you'd rather not face it. My friend Dave cared enough about me that he was willing to share an experience he would have preferred to avoid.

Compassion is not something I control: I either have it for someone or I don't. While Jesus asked us to treat everyone as we would want to be treated, at times he was also "moved with compassion" to engage specific people. That's so desperately needed in a society lost in its work, responsibilities, or favorite media, and one with so few meaningful friendships. We're becoming increasingly isolated with superficial relationships when our hearts desire so much more.

I trust God to bring people across my path that he wants me to know, especially as I follow his nudges to be in places that allow me to interact with others. But it takes some intentionality on our part to move beyond the customary "Hi, how are you?" and open the door to real relationships. Living in God's affection will lead you to ever more spacious places to care about others with an expanded heart. You won't fear as much the hurt people can cause you, and you'll find yourself caring for those who are marginalized in your culture. You'll be less aware of your needs and the expectations of others, and find yourself loving freely.

When you find others who are also doing the same, you'll see his church taking shape around you.

I take special note of those relationships, cultivate them where I can, and see what God might invite us to share together. I don't try to make a group of them, though, because that would take it down another path. I simply enjoy them as family and introduce them to others I know who live similarly. This growing network of friends and friends of friends who can love well creates the kind of environment where people can struggle where they need to struggle, question what they need to question, explore what they need to explore…and share that same freedom with others.

Trust

"How much of what you did in your congregation was motivated by fear?" Six months after my last pastorate I was asked that question by some newfound friends in Australia. I was tempted to say *nothing,* since I didn't consider myself a particularly fearful person. But I thought it best to ask first what he meant.

"Well, how much of what you did was because you were afraid God wouldn't be pleased, how others might force their agenda, who might fall through the cracks, or how others might hurt your reputation in the community?"

"If that's the criteria," I answered with an embarrassed chuckle, "probably ninety percent."

"You're more honest than most," he said and joined my laughter. "Almost all policies are fear-based, trying to protect someone or something. So you know well the 'church' that fear builds. You have yet to discover the church that grows out of trust."

I still remember the awe that overtook me at that moment. I didn't feel rebuked, but as if someone opened a door to a wider space. It had never occurred to me that so much of what I called "church life" had been grounded in fear. I couldn't even envision a church that growing trust in Jesus might produce. Though I claimed to have faith in a generalized sense, I knew I didn't trust God well with anything I couldn't control.

At the time I saw faith as a mental conviction I needed to conjure up to get God to do what I thought best, but that's a far cry from real faith. The reason John wrote his gospel was so that his readers "may believe that Jesus is the Christ, the Son of God, and that by believing have life in his name." (John 2:30-31) I grew up thinking that verse was about theology. Only those who believe the doctrine that Jesus is the Christ will get life. He's actually saying something very different. He's not asking for our doctrinal stand here, but whether or not we trust him enough to believe and follow him. That's the road to life.

Like love, trust isn't a theology or discipline; it's a reality. Where I trust him I get to live free in his care. Where I don't, I end up focused on myself with the attendant anxiety, stress, and insecurity that it provokes. That's why Jesus kept talking to the disciples about faith, encouraging them to trust the Father's care for them. This is the growing edge of every believer's life—learning to trust his love as life unfolds. So whenever I'm caught by anxiety or stress, trust invites me back to him. *What is it about you I don't know, and that if I knew, I would trust you here.*

I don't try to make myself trust him more. I realized a long time ago that trust is not a choice; it is the byproduct of love. When I know someone loves me enough to lay down their life for me, I trust them. Though Jesus already has laid down his life for us, it is easy to forget that in the heat of the moment. Unfortunately, we've trusted our own wisdom and strength longer than we've trusted his. Learning to trust him is not an on/off switch; it's a rheostat. It doesn't change overnight, but grows throughout our lives. The more we get to know him the freer we are to trust. Then we'll find ourselves in circumstances that used to distress us and discover that they no longer do.

The shared journey of growing trust is critical to the new creation community. People who put the focus back on what we should be doing for God destroy that trust. To trust more requires growth in the relationship, and that's what real fellowship encourages. Being near people who are growing in trust and focused on Jesus' work in their lives will encourage your own journey. You don't come away condemned, but more confident of his ability to walk with you through your most difficult moments. That allows us to love people right where they are in their own journey, without trying to push them toward our expectations.

Rest

Religious obligation is an incredibly driven environment with pushy people who advance its ambitions. You know the type. They always know what's best for you and if you don't agree with them they are easily hurt or they get angry and defensive. They want three-hour prayer meetings and an endless array of outreach events. They put pressure on others to join them. If they are in positions of authority, they will use their "giftedness" to bully others with fear and guilt to do what they are "supposed" to do. They quickly cut people off who ask questions or do not conform. How can the church of Jesus flourish there?

The invitation of Jesus was to shed the yoke of our own performance and find what Eugene Peterson so eloquently called "the unforced rhythms of grace" in *The Message*. (Matthew 11:28–30) We can help others find a life in him that allows them not only to receive God's grace, but also to live by that grace through whatever circumstances they face. The third fruit of growing in the Father's affection is to come to rest from our own efforts and ambitions and thus the need to pressure others as well. As love leads to trust, trust leads to rest. We no longer have to force our way because we're confident that he is working things out in ways we can't see.

The writer of Hebrews (chapters 3-4) said a "Sabbath rest" was still available to God's people. He wasn't talking about a day off once a week, but a way of living where we rest from our labors to be part of his. With no need to make our mark on the world, to prove ourselves, or to push others to do what they think best we can more easily see what he is doing.

This is a hard lesson for those who see rest only as an excuse to be lazy. They think nothing gets done when people are at rest, when the truth is that more fruit that counts come from people at rest than from all our frustration and our innate need to "do something great for God." Those who follow God not because they have to but because they delight to are infectious in the world. The most fruitful moments I've had have come when I am least aware of the impact my actions are having on others around me. Walking into a speaking engagement in Australia, I sat down next to a mother whose baby at that moment had just spit out her pacifier. I reached down to grab it and handed it back to the mother with a smile, having no idea that others were watching me. When people found out later I was their speaker, that simple act that seemed so natural for me spoke louder than all the words I used later.

The word for *meekness* in Scripture pictures a warhorse at rest. It doesn't thrash around the paddock snorting and kicking to intimidate the other horses. It stands at the quiet, ready at its master's beck and call to be swift on the run and courageous in battle. Exhaustion and burn-out are certain signs that I'm missing the unforced rhythms of grace and being driven by my own needs. Participating in what God desires may be strenuous at times, and it may even wear us out, but it's a good kind of tired that renews us internally. When the disciples came looking for Jesus with the lunch Jesus had sent them to get, he was no longer hungry. After spending time with the woman at a well he was nourished at a level that even satisfied his physical hunger. (John 4:32–34)

People who live in his rest can share life with others untainted by their agendas and ambitions. They don't have to keep busy to mask their emptiness, or fight for their vision over someone else's. Instead they trust him to build his church and that puts them in the best possible place to collaborate freely with others as Jesus touches the world around them. That's why rest is such a critical component to shared life in his church.

10 | The Family Way

For this reason I kneel before the Father, from whom his whole family in heaven and on earth derives its name.

EPHESIANS 3:14-15

How would you feel going into a staff meeting you were required to attend with a demanding boss? Contrast that with how you'd feel arriving at a family picnic filled with people you love, who know how to enjoy as well as care for one another?

In the first case, I'd be filled with dread and going in I would already be looking forward to the moment it ends. The latter brings a smile to my face with an anticipation of the stories and laughter we'd share. Now, which do you think more accurately reflects the church Jesus is building? What a grave mistake we make when we try to cram the life of the church into an institutional environment! What makes for an efficient organization is completely at odds with how a healthy family thrives.

I understand why we keep doing it. We want to make people pleasing to God, so we create a system of doctrines and activities and build a "church" worthy of him. What we haven't seemed to consider is that at the very attempt to force God's people into a corporate model they become less his people and less reflective of his nature. Families, especially an extended one with multiple generations, cannot be constructed or held together by management systems but only by love and the quality of relationships they share together.

His church is family first and foremost. My heart goes out to those who have tried an ever-changing set of systems in hopes of replicating the love and generosity of the early believers only to be frustrated by the results. They had no idea they were putting so much effort into an environment that could not achieve their vision. The most pastoral among them could never manipulate people in a way that was necessary to build a successful organization. While they thought themselves failures, they were perhaps the most successful people in the room. They loved people too much to exploit them by plugging them into a machine.

Once we create an environment, define the rules by which it works, and then encourage people to conform, we lose the spirit of that family. There's a reason why dysfunctional families and shattered relationships hurt so deeply. We were created for something better. We are designed for connection and sharing a depth of love others can rely on. That's why it is so destructive when a parent neglects, abuses, or abandons their children; when a spouse betrays their marriage; or when sibling relationships are marked by conflict and competition. There is enough betrayal, deceit, exploitation, and conflict in our broken world. The church is a haven from that, not another place to play the game.

Seemingly, we haven't learned that yet because we continually seek the right system to manage our life together. Throughout our history we have tried many schemes hoping that our corporate decisions will reflect God's will. Very early on, local bishops took on nearly autocratic power. Eventually that evolved into a hierarchy of bishops, which claimed apostolic succession dating back to Peter. Not only did this claim have significant gaps, but it also germinated a leadership bureaucracy that is foreign to Scripture. Other denominations have tried the same approach and fared no better. In more recent centuries, many congregations have opted for more local determination to utilize either a council of elders or democratic voting of the membership. Today the single elder/senior pastor model puts authority in the lap of someone supposedly anointed to represent Jesus to the local community.

The fact that all of them claim a Scriptural basis might lead us to believe that Scripture doesn't clearly offer one. Not surprisingly, each of these styles reflect the cultural trends of their day. The hierarchy of bishops is just royalty cloaked in Christian garb. Congregational forms emerged at the same time royalty was being dislodged by democratic movements. The strong-armed senior pastor is a copy of the corporate CEO, who can cast a vision and reward those who follow.

All of these forms are grounded in the old creation where power is negotiated to find out who gets to decide what is God's will for others. Those in power want us to believe that the process itself guarantees that they speak for Jesus and that the faithful must follow. It doesn't take much discernment to realize that none of these leadership models guarantee that the people holding positions in them are following Jesus. While the people behind them may be well intentioned, they have failed to note just how much organizations take on a life of their own in serving the needs of leadership to run an efficient program and to obtain the resources necessary to sustain it.

The early church seemed less concerned with finding the right process than with whether they reached the right outcome. As we saw earlier when the elders in Ephesus were no longer responding to the head of the church, John wrote them as a reminder that they each had an anointing from the Spirit to know what's true instead of having to trust unfaithful elders. I realize how incomprehensible that is for people who see the church as a human institution. It would lead to chaos. But if the church isn't an institution at all, then there is no need to demand conformity. People will either follow him freely or they will pursue their own ambitions. That kind of freedom is essential to growth; in time the fruit of their lives will demonstrate their pursuit.

So, instead of banking on a process we claim to be biblical, let's begin instead with the outcome itself. Jesus is the head of the church, as he is the head of every life in it. When people follow him they don't have to be managed, their personal agendas fade away, and love runs deep. Most us have been part of incredible moments like that and know how transcendent they can be. We also know how quickly it fades away as soon as someone tries to control it.

Extravagant love—not imposed order—is the nature of his church. That's why his church is a family: a Father inviting us to take our place in his home; an older brother, Jesus, who empathizes with our struggles and offers us grace in time of need; a Spirit who empowers us; and brothers and sisters who can live alongside us with love and honor. The church reflects the best of what a family can be. It is less concerned with conformity than it is with creating a safe environment where people can be open and honest, even confessional, because they know we are all in the struggle together. Its people won't have to boast about their strengths nor hide weaknesses, and others won't try to fix them with advice or tell them what they should think or how they should feel.

In the old creation, people tend to be more self-focused: trying to be loved, rather than loving. They are more preoccupied with meetings and activities than they are with sharing friendship. The relationships they do have are mostly task-based, and only last as long as they are working or meeting together. The family way, however, encourages friendships to flourish because people enjoy being together and genuinely care about one another. They share laughter even through difficult circumstances. They serve one another in times of need, and that even extends to strangers in need who cross their paths.

Religious settings are laced with guilt and fear as people constantly question whether they are doing enough for God. They employ the language of accountability and pressure people to live up to the expectations they ascribe to God. People have to pretend to be better than they are in order to please the leadership and stay out of trouble.

A healthy family, however, doesn't press people to perform even under the illusion that it is for their own good. Those who know Jesus know that he invites people into his life; he does not force them. While a healthy relationship is encouraging, there is no compulsion to make others do what isn't in their heart to do. Authenticity and the freedom of each person's conscience is cherished. They respect each other's journey in the full confidence that you will open to truth faster when you are not coerced.

Those who serve God out of fear and obligation have no such confidence. They are critical when others fall short, constantly attack those who think differently, and arrogantly push their views on others. The environment that spawns is argumentative and compulsive, full of demands that people commit to and are obligated to follow their program. In the new creation people value friendship over achievement and will fight to save relationships through confession, forgiveness, and reconciliation. They accept the fact that we are all flawed and will make mistakes as we learn to follow him and relate to others. They know being right with one another is more important than being right about an issue.

Human-centered environments are managed by the experts and become incredibly competitive, as people want to be in charge and grab the spotlight. Gossip runs riot as people jockey for position in formal and informal hierarchies. A healthy family, however, inculcates a collaborative environment: people working and growing together. They share openly, offering whatever they have without a thought to what they'll get in return. They demonstrate humility and respect because they have nothing to prove and nothing to gain in one-upping others. They trust the Spirit to work as he wills, and they can support each other even if they don't see eye-to-eye on everything.

They know that the joy of family is found in laying their lives down for others. Jesus told his disciples that life comes by serving others and not by getting them to serve us. Nothing more clearly reveals Jesus' family than when people are loved, not used. Every other human environment is laced with people trying to get ahead and willing to use relationships to their own advantage. After the success of *The Shack,* people came out of the woodwork to seek my help with their book or project. Few of those I talked to had any desire for a friendship; they only wanted to use my gifts or connections. People who know Jesus are not manipulative and care more for the people involved than advancing their agenda.

This environment levels the playing field. No one lords it over anyone else. Jesus made that clear in Matthew 23 when he told the original disciples: "But you are not to be called 'Rabbi,' for you have one Teacher, and you are all brothers. And do not call anyone on earth 'father,' for you have one Father, and he is in heaven." Even though Paul didn't hear Jesus expressly forbid the language of leadership to his followers, it would appear he got the memo. Paul's entire orientation toward the church was as a brother among the family. Though Paul used the language of elders and overseers, he does so less than two dozen times, and then only as a function, never as a title or position. More than 120 times Paul uses the language of family—brothers, sisters, and joint-heirs.

Those who do not trust Jesus to build his church cannot imagine church life without leaders and followers. They will use all kinds of proof texts to justify it, but the heart of their argument is not in the new creation. In chapter eighteen, we'll talk more about how the gifts people have to build up others are best shared alongside them rather than above them.

Of course no one learns to live this reality overnight, and as relationships shift and change we'll make constant adjustments to allow his church to take shape around us. It isn't a switch you can turn on or even something you can pretend for very long. Learning to respond to the transforming power of his love is a process. It helps me to think of it like the noise-to-signal ratio we had to negotiate in tuning an analog TV or radio signal. Instead of entering a digital channel and getting clear reception, we had to dial in to that sweet spot where the signal was crisp and clear. Depending how far we were from the station, that often required fine-tuning and even then we couldn't get rid of all the static. At those times you just hoped for enough signal so that the noise wasn't too distracting.

In the next eight chapters we're going to look at a series of contrasts between the way humans work and the way God's family does. Though I'll state these contrasts in extreme terms to help you see the distinction, we will need to keep in mind that no environment is going to be perfect. It is going to be more like a family and less like a business, more a growing network of friends than a set of rules and rituals.

These are growing characteristics to look for as you seek to identify how Jesus' church is taking shape around you and how you can engage it. Don't look for people living them perfectly and don't try to pretend you can do so yourself. I share them only to help you learn to zero in on the signal of his love and grace as you tune out the noise of human manipulation. I am well aware that we can try to turn these into objectives and try to replicate the environment by human effort. Doing so will not only fail to achieve the reality but exhaust us in the process. Like so much of this kingdom, one can only learn to detect his reality by experiencing enough of him that he shapes the way we live. That happens both by recognizing where he is working and the fruit that results, as well as by growing weary of the futility and frustration of our own agenda.

The church Jesus is building will defy all human attempts to replicate it because it is the fruit of a life well loved. It is simply the way people share life together when Jesus is their growing preoccupation and they are learning to listen and follow him. If people are not on that journey there is no way to organize them into anything that looks like his church. The reason I take such pains to help people learn to live in the Father's affection is so they can not only know him but also experience the reality of his church taking shape among humanity.

As we freely love the people God has put around our lives, it will become evident who is able to share that love in return. That's the church taking shape. For those who aren't in that place yet, wouldn't we be better off spending our time loving them into that relationship, rather than forcing them to play by the rules? In other words, I'm not looking to limit people's access to "my group" so I can preserve the purity of the church. That's Jesus' job. We don't exclude people as if church life is a privilege we portion out. People exclude themselves by their behavior. The three-year-old throwing a tantrum can't participate in the life of the family until she exhausts her attempts to control it.

Those who don't know they're loved need our affection, not our judgment and rejection. They may first see it reflected in the way we care for them, and then they will come to see it from the Source himself. I simply get to do what Jesus asks and love those who cross my path, as he has loved me. If they are free enough to share church life together, then I'm going to enjoy getting to know them. If they are not free enough yet, I'm going to find a way to love them that will open that door to them. And I will enjoy that, too.

As his love wins you, you will find yourself increasingly free to share in the life of his family. That's how Jesus said the kingdom would make its way into the world—not by human activity or religious practice, but watching love reveal itself in a growing circle of friends and friends of friends. Everything God needs to accomplish on earth will be achieved through loving others the way he loved us. That's the promise of John 13. The shared life of the church is an environment where love prepares the way for truth and light to embrace people into the reality of the new creation.

We don't have to find a church, or plant one. This is a family to engage, not a program to implement. Defining a program destroys the family. Wouldn't it be better if we simply recognized the relationships in which church life is already being expressed and give time and attention to them? Paul said it is God's task to place each of us in the body as he desires. (I Corinthians 12:18) He does that best when we're not trying to plot our own way in or get from others what we think we might need.

So what are the telltale signs of the church that rise out of Jesus' new creation? Each of the next eight chapters will highlight a different characteristic that can help you tune in to his reality and let the noise of religious obligation fade away. Then, you too can see his church taking shape around you.

11 | In First Place...

And he is the head of the body, the church...
so that in everything he might have the
supremacy.

COLOSSIANS 1:18

Characteristic One:
Jesus himself is the overwhelming focus.

Those who don't understand the power of Jesus' kind of love often make the charge that it is just warm fuzzy feelings and people trying to be nice to each other. They mock it as weak and ineffectual because they know you can't run an efficient organization without effective command and control. While that's true if you're speaking about the old creation, it is not true in his kingdom because his church only functions where Jesus gets first place in all things and where whatever is broken in our world gets restored in his.

Governments are how we attempt to manage human frailty and weakness. For most of our history, governance has simply allowed the strong to force their way on the weak. In many ways it still does, even in our democratic societies. Though it ostensibly exists to build a free society at home and a respectful peace with other societies, those hopes are quickly thwarted by the inequities of human culture, the greed for power and money that corrupts its leaders, and the darker side of human ambition that seeks its own gain above a common good. A brief look at the news on any day will easily confirm just how damaged and divided human culture is with its persistent parade of wars, crime, lawsuits, broken homes, and damaged relationships due to the quest for control.

Almost everyone, somewhere deep inside, yearns for something better. Why can't people be gracious, treating others kindly, honestly, and fairly while caring about them as much as they care about their own needs? While that would seem simple enough on the surface, it seems to ask more of people than they have to give. Left to ourselves we will process every situation in light of our own gain. Until the power of self and shame is laid to rest in the human heart, we cannot live differently in the world and its systems, be they religious or political. They will eventually become just another tool to further our ambitions and manage our fears.

God never intended for us to live in such conflict and isolation. His desire has always been for a world where genuine affection and concern for others replace our selfish ambition. From the beginning it has been his purpose to bring everything that sin separated, including heaven and earth, into one glorious, new whole. He wasn't the author of conflict or violence, but the one seeking to rescue the creation from its brokenness. His plan was to bring "everything together under Jesus himself." (Ephesians 1:9-10) Where does that begin? Inside each and every human heart that allows him to begin to untwist the powers of self and shame so that we no longer fall victim to our insecurities. Where we trust his unfolding purpose we will no longer fight for our own, and when his desires become ours we'll find a growing unity with others who are also living in that new creation. This is the community our hearts long for, a society that lives outside the human need to manage power.

That society is the church of Jesus Christ. It's the people growing to know him, love like him, and reflect his passion to bring all things together, not to continue the same conflict and one-upmanship reflected in the old creation. Unfortunately what has been identified as "the church" for two thousand years has often contributed more to the brokenness of our world than to its healing by engaging in division, conflict, and even war. I stood on a hill in Ireland where one of the great battles had been fought between the British and the Irish in the fight for independence. My guide that day told me that each of the armies had gathered on the previous night for a prolonged service to ask God to bless them and give them victory over their enemies. God has often been the victim of such prayers.

Obviously it is one thing to confess Christ as the head of his church, and quite another to live as if he is. If what we call the church had been following Jesus during the past two thousand years, we would see it as a significant voice that invites people to freedom in Christ and brings people together under a banner of his love and life. But the opposite has been true. The trajectory of Christian history during two millennia has not been toward greater love and unity but to greater division, suspicion, and animosity. While Christianity held together under one institution for its first one thousand years, it was embedded in constant conflict and corruption, always in need of reform. But institutions prove rigid to change and that's especially true of larger and longer-established ones. Instead of listening to its critics, it tortured them back into line or, failing that, executed them.

The reason we don't see one flock today is because we have hundreds of thousands of would-be shepherds leading people to follow their mission, vision, or program. Jesus said we'd be one flock when we have one shepherd. (John 10:16) As long as we have thousands of men and women claiming to lead on his behalf and ensuring loyalty to themselves and their program we will find ourselves in conflict with God's goal to bring all things together in him. Imagine the church we would see today if Christians throughout the centuries had taken the effort and resources used to set up, manage, and pay for their institutions and invested them instead in learning to love people in a way that bore witness to his reality. Instead, we've ended up with structures that value religion over relationship, icons over substance, and conformity over relational transformation. The unholy alliance between an institution's need for conformity and our ability to distort God's image to compel people by fear or guilt seems a greater temptation than humanity can resist.

While every Christian pledges allegiance to Jesus as the head of the church and his image adorns our buildings and trinkets, following him has been trickier. In its earliest days, the church forgot that Isaiah prophesied that the government would rest on *his* shoulders (Isaiah 9:6), not ours. When we undertake to lead others on his behalf, we supplant him as the Head of the church in deference to our own best wisdom and desires. It does for the church what the Old Testament kings did for Israel. Those who lead become victims of their own power, overindulgent to their every whim, and exploitive of those they were meant to serve.

When Ezekiel castigated the worthless shepherds of Israel (Ezekiel 33), declaring God would remove them from their place, he didn't say that God would replace them with better shepherds. He said that God would shepherd his own people and they would never be afraid again. Jesus reiterated that in John 10. He declared himself the Good Shepherd and said that his sheep would recognize his voice and follow him instead of the hireling who would only look out for his own needs. The point of these two passages seems to be that shepherding people is too significant a task to entrust to broken humanity and the New Covenant would allow Jesus to do it himself. That's why the invitation in the Gospel was to "Come, follow me," not to follow the book or religious leaders.

Where Jesus is in first place, the church thrives. That's not a place we give him of course. He already has it. Our recognition of it allows us to see the church he is building. In the words of Eugene Peterson, Jesus gets "the last word on everything and everyone." (I Peter 3:22, *The Message*) Whatever horror has been done in the world and whatever injustice you suffered, Jesus will get the last word. Too often it looks like people who cut corners succeed and those who cause pain get away with it. But that is only how it appears. When he sets things right no pain will go unhealed and no injustice ignored.

Though he may not yet have had the last word in circumstances that concern you, he will. What we get to do now is learn to live in him and join him in the new creation, even while he resolves our brokenness in the old creation. That will not mean he fixes every circumstance the way we want, or immediately bring the justice we hope for, but he will heal us and lead us into more spacious places of living in him.

If you want to find his church, learn to live under the supremacy of Jesus and look for others who share that preoccupation as well. His purpose will be their motivation, his character their ideal, following him their greatest desire. While they are still involved in this age—family, work, weather, politics, sports, and recreation—people engaged with Jesus always find the conversation turning back toward him and what he's doing in them. Each person has a growing life in Jesus and that naturally comes out when they're together, the things they are seeing that have touched them as well as the questions and struggles they're still sorting through. I come away from these conversations more settled in who Jesus is and encouraged to draw more closely to him.

That's the signal of church life. Static increases where people are focused on doctrinal controversies, programs, or activities. When someone tries to bring up spiritual things in that context the conversation will feel artificial and soon fade out after a comment or two. That's why the institutional answers here are not easy. Once we institutionalize God's working, a host of factors come into play that make it difficult to keep Jesus in first place. There is no system humanity can design that can't immediately be taken advantage of by those who seek to lead it, and those who seek to benefit from it.

When we make any thing else central to the life of the church, even something good, he is pushed aside, however unwittingly. Within a few centuries attendance at the communion meal became more important than knowing Christ. Over the centuries we've done it with lots of other things including Scripture, "church tradition," the Sunday meeting, or allegiance to a pastor. There is only one cornerstone. When the present, active Jesus is displaced, what remains will reflect more human ambition instead of the purpose of God.

The only way Jesus can stay central is when every life learns how to listen and respond to him. He exercises his headship not through a chain of command but by being the head of every life in it. We acknowledge his place by actually following the Lamb as best we perceive him. That's not a decision you can make once for the rest of your life. It is a continuous challenge in a hundred decisions made day after day as you learn how different his desires are from your own. The new creation is not some sort of spiritual Disneyland where your every dream comes true. It's where Jesus' every word and desire comes to pass.

Our security is found not in any particular expression of church, but by our relationship with him. He's always wanted to be the one to guide us. While teachers can be valuable tools to help us discover a growing life in Jesus, they become valueless if they supplant his ongoing revelation in our hearts. The New Testament is filled with language that invites people into the depth of that relationship, so much so that everyone can know him "from the least of them to the greatest" (Hebrews 8:11), and that "You do not need anyone to teach you..." (I John 2:27)

Of course, the perceived danger is that people who don't have a clue who he is will claim to follow him and simply use his name to justify their ambitions. Without structure to rein them in, some argue, people will simply fall into error. While that may seem true on the surface, it neglects the fact that our institutions fall into error as well. Jesus preferred vesting our security in the Spirit within, rather than human powers without. Those who only claim to follow Jesus will become obvious in time and their damage is far less when others are not forced to follow them.

Can't an institution keep Jesus at the center? Of course it can, but it rarely happens and usually doesn't last long before the institutional structure crowds him out. Our best structures seem to be simple and temporary, designed to accomplish a task rather than to perpetuate themselves after they've outlived their usefulness. It takes incredible courage to admit we've climbed the proverbial ladder that's resting on the wrong wall, and even more to climb off that ladder and find a better wall. That's especially true from those who rent out space on the wall of human ambition. Upton Sinclair described the problem: "It is difficult to get a man to understand something when his salary depends on him not understanding it."

Even our well-intentioned efforts are a distraction to the community Jesus can create when he draws the family to himself. Last weekend someone asked me what I had done as a pastor to help facilitate community among people in my congregation. I struggled to find an answer and ended up concluding he'd perhaps asked the wrong question. "Instead of asking what I did to facilitate it, it might be more accurate to ask what we did to disrupt the community that Jesus was giving us." People did what we asked them as we formed an ever-changing array of home groups to help encourage fellowship. But the ones that worked well did so in spite of our structure. Friendships between people flourished not because of the program, but because people in them had a passion for Jesus that extended into their relationships.

As we learn to live under his headship, the church appears wherever we connect with others. Instead of trying to create it on our own, we simply embrace the relationship and connections he brings to us. Enjoy its reality even as you resist the urge to protect it. As soon as we try to cram the transcendent reality of the church into a human system, its vitality will ebb. That means we'll have to see the church as a bit more liquid than we were taught because it's a reality we recognize, not one we control.

When we unhinge our concept of fellowship from our institutions and pre-planned routines, the possibilities are limitless. Across the globe people are coming alive in his new creation beyond the human systems we are quick to celebrate. In fact Jesus seems to do his best work away from the spotlight humanity values. If your only exposure to what God is doing today is in *Christianity Today, Charisma Magazine,* or Christian television, then you are missing so much that God is doing in our world. If you are looking for your local congregation to report on it, they probably don't see it either.

Jesus is inviting people back to himself, the only true Shepherd of the sheep, and the connections I have found offer the best examples of church life I've ever seen. These people are often despised and accused of rebellion, but that has not deterred them. They are simply learning how to let Jesus have first place in their hearts and how to share his life with love and graciousness. They are not looking for a movement to follow but a temple that is not made with human hands. They are well on their way to seeing it.

12 Not Made with Hands

Are you so foolish? After beginning with the Spirit, are you now trying to attain your goal by human effort?

GALATIANS 3:3

Characteristic Two:
Trusting Jesus' work over human effort.

During my travels I have found myself near the most opulent palaces, castles, and cathedrals in Europe, and I am always fascinated with the scale, architecture, and art that fill those buildings. As impressive as they are, and all the more so that they were built without modern technology, my appreciation is always restrained by the realization that they were built by the enslaved for the benefit of a privileged few. As I stood in the immensity of St. Peter's Basilica in Rome, my stomach churned knowing that many such cathedrals were built on the twisted theology of indulgences and the guilt money it garnered. Obviously if you're building something for God, or at least if you say you are, you spare no expense, especially when you need the grandeur to intimidate the masses with wealth and power.

When I read the Old Testament, however, I get the idea that God doesn't share our penchant for such extravagance. He never asked for a temple to be built, seemingly content with the less permanent tabernacle. But David grew uncomfortable living in a palace while the ark was in a tent and thus decided God needed a more stately home. Though he wasn't allowed to build it, God allowed his son Solomon to do so and it became the focus of Israel's faith.

When Jesus came on the scene he didn't view the temple as an asset for Israel, but as a distraction. It served the illusion that God could be contained in a building, far from the daily lives of those he wanted to engage. It wasn't even a house of prayer anymore but a place of commerce. Jesus found it offensive and upended the tables of the moneychangers declaring, "Destroy this temple, and I will raise it again in three days." (John 20:19)

His words were layered with meaning. The disciples point out that the temple he spoke of was his own body. They would destroy it and he would raise it up in three days. But the religious leaders interpreted these words to mean their temple, and that may have been partly true. Not that he needed them to destroy it physically, but he at least wanted them to destroy what it had come to represent in their minds, that the transcendent God of the universe could be contained in a building, opulent though it may be. He didn't want a palace of gold and silver, but to be at home in the hearts of his people. Yet the idea that God is more present even in the remains of its stone walls is still prevalent today as any visit to the Western Wall will attest.

The tabernacle was not God's true home, much less the temple. It was a contrivance to let Israel think God was among them at some distance, since knowing he was in their tents was more than their shame-based hearts could bear. The Incarnation demonstrated that our fear of God was a perception on our part, rather than what God wanted or deserved. Jesus was among humanity and no one ran away in terror. What God had lost in Eden, he was finding again—a home among his Creation.

The temples, cathedrals, and even our "church" buildings represent the opposite of that reality. They were designed to create a sacred space that would elevate God beyond human engagement, to leave us feeling insignificant in his eyes instead of empowering us to draw near to him in confidence. The Incarnation proved that God wanted to inhabit all of life with us and make our homes, workplaces, and recreation sacred because he would be with us in them.

That was Stephen's point when he declared to the mob ready to kill him, "The Most High does not live in houses made by men." (Acts 7:48) Perhaps nothing is more scandalous about the Incarnation than that the holy God could live joyfully among broken humanity, and nothing more amazing about the New Covenant than that God wanted to take up residence in the human heart. Jesus never wanted an opulent building to be the enduring image of his church. He wanted a living temple made up of men and women from all over the world who have abandoned their agendas to embrace his.

You are…fellow citizens with God's people and members of God's household, built on the foundation of the apostles and prophets, with Christ Jesus himself as the chief cornerstone. In him the whole building is joined together and rises to become a holy temple in the Lord. And in him you too are being built together to become a dwelling in which God lives by his Spirit. (Ephesians 2:19-22)

This is no physical building that Paul describes; it's just the metaphor. For the first three hundred years of the church's existence, no one thought of the church as a building and no one thought to build one. His temple is alive, beginning in an individual's heart and then knit into a worldwide network of interconnected lives whose very relationships put on display the glory of the Lord. There's no way human effort can build that, and all our attempts have fallen woefully short.

This is a long-running theme in Scripture. God wants to invite us into his reality and we keep trying to create our own for him. It started in a garden with Adam and Eve's desire for knowledge apart from their relationship with him. It continued when Israel wanted a king rather than to trust God to lead them. Whenever they were under threat they counted horses and chariots to measure their chances in battle, unable to believe that God with them was greater than all the resources they could muster. Now the focus is on the church, and whether or not we truly believe it is something only Jesus can build.

More than a decade ago I was sitting with a good friend discussing some of the new books being put out in the Christian marketplace. One in particular held some views about the church similar to what my friend and I share, but it was packaged in a way that seemed to undermine the priorities the author sought to encourage. In the middle of sorting through what we liked and didn't like about it, my friend looked up at me and said, "It just doesn't have the fragrance of Father about it, does it?"

And that's when the lights went on. No, it didn't. The writer had subtly replaced the work of Jesus in the human heart with his own system, biblical though he claimed it to be, and all it would take to implement would be a group of people following the right principles. Though it may not have been his intent, he took some important truths about the nature of the church and separated them from trusting in the One who is Truth itself. Without his active engagement all the truth we know will go unrealized. We'll simply be left to our own well-intentioned effort to try and do something great for God that in the end will not bear his glory.

Finding the fragrance of Father in the circumstances that surround me has been my passion ever since. I have more opportunities surrounding my life than I have time to pursue, and it has been helpful to step back and determine whether an opportunity before me exudes the sweet scent of Father's nature or the telltale odor of human sweat. I don't always get it right, to be sure, but looking for that fragrance has helped me look beyond what I want or what I think is right and follow what he desires.

Nowhere is that more important than in discovering our place in the church Jesus is building. Our overestimation of human ingenuity and capability to build something great for God continues to take us down the side road of our own efforts and miss the glory of his greater working. For it's not just our buildings that seek to contain him, so too do our traditions, doctrines, and disciplines. He does not live in buildings made with hands or in systems designed by human ingenuity. How many times have you completed yet another class or workbook that talked about God, but didn't help you come to know him?

That describes my first twenty years of vocational ministry. There was so much I could do for God that it took me decades to realize that my best ideas coupled with my most ardent efforts could not accomplish God's desires. Perhaps that's the greatest difference Paul experienced in transitioning from a hardworking Pharisee to his freedom in the life of Jesus. Afterward he "put no confidence in the flesh" even though he had quite the résumé. He had come to realize that the works of God were beyond his abilities. Even though he had kept the rules the Pharisees had contrived to fulfill the law, it didn't make him righteous. It only pushed his sin deeper where it revealed itself in arrogance, blasphemy, and murder.

Most have a natural aversion to the treadmill of religious performance, but I was not among them. I could work it well and get accolades for doing so. I used to think it was because I was more radically committed to Jesus than the slackers around me. Now I know that motive was mixed with a more selfish desire to climb to the top of the Christian mountain. Regretfully, for many years I had the strength of will to pull it off, which allowed me to feast on the illusion that I was better than others, unaware that the pride of self-righteousness is even more destructive than unrighteousness.

That's why Paul concluded he only wanted the righteousness that comes from a growing trust in God. The more he came to know Jesus, the more his selfish ambitions came untangled. Like him, overachievers need their own pharisectomy, where their inner Pharisee gets cut away. I'll warn you, it's not a quick procedure. I'm in the twentieth year of my pharisectomy as I write this. Any confidence in my flesh is sorely misplaced, whether it is indulging in sin or the impulse to do God's work for him. The new creation thrives where we simply respond to what he is doing in us each day, as the great tapestry of his purpose unfolds. The failure of humanity through the ages is to live as if God is not with us and as if he does not love us.

If we can't trust him with our own lives, how will we ever trust him to build his church and bring us to unity in a way that will threaten the worldly powers of this age? Jesus told Nicodemus (John 3) that the Spirit works differently from the way humans do, and people trying to figure it out from the outside will only grow frustrated. Following him is less like following a four-point plan as it is catching a ride on the wind. To experience that reality Jesus told Nicodemus he would have to be born all over again. He couldn't add this new creation to his old religious mind-set. He would need to abandon his own ideas to learn how to follow a life-giving Spirit.

If you don't know the power of growing trust, I know how impossible this all sounds. I grew up hearing, "If we won't, God can't" and that "we are his hands extended." If we don't get busy and do something, nothing will happen. Most people think the idea that "God helps those who help themselves" is in the Bible. It isn't. It's an ancient Greek proverb often credited to Benjamin Franklin. The reason it endures is because that's what religion teaches us and we can't imagine what we would do if we weren't driven by fear or obligation. The urge to "do something" when we feel insecure is the driving force behind much of our fruitless busyness.

"So we just sit around and do nothing?" I've heard that question countless times when helping people learn to find freedom from fear and obligation. Trust is so meaningless to them that they think of it as fatalism—God does everything while we sit silently by. How wrong they are; that kind of thinking is the result of years of doing things *for* God instead of doing things *with* him.

The opposite of living confident in human effort is not lethargy but living in a growing trust in who God is and what he is doing around you. That can lead to seasons of arduous labor, excruciating pain, and overwhelming need. Paul said that his desire to present everyone mature in Christ led him to "strenuously contend with all the energy Christ so powerfully works in me." (Colossians 1:29) Elsewhere he said he was "under great pressure, far beyond our ability to endure, so that we despaired of life itself." (2 Corinthians 1:8)

Participating in God's purpose will make you incredibly active, but it's just a different kind of activity. Instead of striking out to do what we think best and asking him to bless it, we learn how to sense what he is already doing around us and join him there. Since writing *So You Don't Want to Go to Church Anymore*, the most frequent question I'm asked by those who missed the point of the book is, "What should the church look like?" Here's an example: "Like you, we have given up on the institutional church and are wondering what guidance you can give us about starting something new. How do groups start? Is there a model we can use successfully in this way? I am excited at the thought of what this might look like, but we don't want to do it the wrong way."

My answer is usually, "Resist the urge to start anything." Our two thousand year history has made us look to models and forms, rather than learning to trust him and live in concert with others as he leads us. Anything we start will invariably be focused on the type, frequency, and location of meetings, or the role of leadership to manage the group. Our underlying assumption is that there must be a formula we can follow to replicate church whenever we want. Wouldn't you think if such a model existed, Jesus would have shared it with us?

As long as we are seeking to implement a model, we are not following him. I've seen incredible demonstrations of the life of the church among people all over the world, and they have one thing in common. They are not trying to imitate someone's system; they are simply following him and enjoying the relationships God gives them. As those friendships grow they learn how to care for one another and do the simple things God might ask them to do together without creating permanent systems or commitments to replace the relationship. They realize God works in seasons and establishing rituals is how we minimize our dependence on him.

While most of these people who want to start something sincerely want to experience the life of the church, they are just approaching it backward. Jesus is already building his church and he is too creative to have a standard process that fits all people in every location. Each of us is unique and in different places in our journeys. Why would we assume there's a standard process that will fit any collection of people? When the focus is on the relationships he's inviting us into, rather than the group we want to form, we'll be focused on the more important part—how do we live in and share his love? It's about relationships, not structures; friendships, not meetings. If you haven't tasted that yet, a most amazing adventure awaits.

Seeing his church bring all things together without adding our human systems may sound impossible, especially in light of all the religious structures that fill the earth. But she is already in process and her outcome certain. A few years ago I toured the Apartheid Museum in Johannesburg, South Africa. I was stunned by the juxtaposition of two video recordings being played on video screens sitting next to each other. In the mid-1980s, South African society was coming apart as an increasing number of blacks demanded the right to vote and participate in the democratic process.

At one point, a reporter thrusts a microphone in the face of the president of South Africa, P. W. Botha, asking him if one-man, one-vote rule will ever come to South Africa. Standing on the steps of an opulent government building, his pompous chest swelled with defiance as he scowled with complete confidence, he declared, "Never!"

On the next monitor Winnie Mandela, who was at the time the wife of political prisoner and eventual president Nelson Mandela, ran from the police through a haze of tear gas. A reporter called out to her with the same question that had been posed to President Botha. She paused in the melee to turn toward the camera, "Ah," she said as a smile broke out across her face. Even though all the powers of the state were arrayed against her and her fellow demonstrators, her confidence was clear: "It is inevitable!"

And so it was!

Will the church Jesus is building be fully revealed in the earth? It is inevitable.

God's temple is rising in the world. It may be obscured at times by organizations claiming to be the church, but whose actions smell more of human flesh than the fragrance of a loving Father. In the long run it just may be that the history of Christianity to date is not so different from Old Testament history, where moments of God's revelation are followed by years of unfaithfulness to his ways, while we give more credence to our own.

But his temple keeps rising. Each added person only reflects his multifaceted glory with more accuracy and will confound the wisdom of the world by the power of its love and the simplicity of its life. Wherever people are learning to live in his love and love others, the temple rises. Whenever people learn to listen to him instead of the manipulative voices of religious leaders, the temple rises. However people find ways to work together by laying their lives down in kindness and generosity, the temple rises.

Its completion is inevitable because Jesus is the one building it. It cannot be made with hands because it isn't made of brick and mortar. It can't be drawn up on a flow chart because it isn't a system. It is a living organism made up of all the people who recognize the supremacy of Jesus. This has been his purpose since the first act of creation: His intent was that now, through the church, the manifold wisdom of God should be made known to the rulers and authorities in the heavenly realms, according to his eternal purpose that he accomplished in Christ Jesus our Lord. (Ephesians 3:10-11)

13 | Devotion without Obligation

Your people will volunteer freely in the day of your power...

PSALM 110:3 NAS

Characteristic Three:
Community grows from the desire of a transformed heart.

No one misunderstands the reality of the church Jesus is building more than those who say others must attend a local congregation even if they find the experience distasteful or boring.

That crosses my mind every time I hear that Christians "have to go to a church" because we "need fellowship." Is that why they go, because they have to? That thinking has become so ubiquitous in Christian circles that attendance at a congregation has become the litmus test to measure the sincerity of someone's faith. And since the early believers didn't see church life as an obligation to a meeting, we have to twist Scripture to try and prove the point:

Your love for one another will prove to the world that you are my disciples'. The Bible says a Christian without a church home is like an organ without a body, a sheep without a flock, or a child without a family. It is an unnatural state.... Except for a few important exceptions referring to all believers throughout history, almost every time the word "church" is used in the Bible it refers to a local, visible congregation. The New Testament assumes membership in a local congregation. A church family identifies you as a genuine believer. (*A Church Family Identifies You As a Believer* by Rick Warren, in the August 29, 2012, Daily Hope Devotional)

Here Mr. Warren begins with a true statement. Our love for others will demonstrate to the world that Jesus lives in us. Then watch how subtly he replaces the call to love others with being a member of a local congregation. That's quite a leap! And then he makes the wild assertion that every time the word "church" is used in Scripture it's referring to one of those same institutions.

Many, like Warren, assume that Jesus' command wasn't really to love each other, it was just a coded way to say "go to church" on Sunday morning. You can't love people by talking to them and caring for them, but only by sitting silently in a pew beside them. Put like that, doesn't it sound a bit crazy? Do people really think that when Jesus told us to love each other, he meant we had to join a local congregation to do it, especially when their priorities differ so vastly from what Jesus asked of us? Am I missing something here?

The truth is, I missed something here for a long time. I used to teach the same nonsense, that the only way to be part of his church was to attend a sanctioned congregation. I regarded with suspicion those who did not belong to a local fellowship. It was easier to dismiss them as hurt, bitter, or independent than it was to wrestle with the idea that our congregation could be irrelevant to people who were deeply passionate about Jesus. I've since discovered that attending a local congregation has little to do with whether or not someone is coming to know him or whether they are connected to his church.

In fact, making attendance an obligation may already demonstrate that we've lost the vitality of real community and have become mired in mundane rituals, demands for conformity, or internal conflicts that alienate people. Jesus talked about his kingdom being a pearl of great price. If people saw its reality, they would give up anything to be part of it. Living in him and sharing that life with others isn't drudgery. It fulfills the deepest longings of the human heart.

If you're looking for Jesus' church, look for people who are drawn together by their passion for God and one another, not those who talk about commitment and accountability. Who wouldn't have wanted to be at that lunch with Zaccheus, in some of those boat conversations crossing the Sea of Galilee, or in Bethany having a meal with Lazarus, Mary, and Martha? Being with Jesus among a group of people watching him love them into his reality, spurring them on with his wisdom, or opening doors of trust into their hearts would be a joy. Wouldn't it be unthinkable to be anywhere else?

Wouldn't the same be true of the Day of Pentecost, praying with the disciples in the upper room after two of them had been arrested, or hearing Paul expound the gospel in Lydia's house? If someone had told them they had to "go to church" as an obligation, I think they would have been too bewildered to come up with a response. The unfolding work of God among people is an endearing reality. Why would we turn church participation into an obligation instead of cultivating a life together that rises to the promise of the church being his fullness in the world?

If you had been a fly on the wall in my home this past Sunday, you would have seen a group of people sharing life together. There was plenty laughter and food. People ranged in age from two to sixty with lots of mingling among the various age and interest groups. We never stopped the flow of relationship to hold a meeting where everyone had to stop and pay attention to one person, but there was plenty of conversation, some of it with deep prayer and concern. If you had watched the day unfold, you might have assumed we had all been good friends for a long time, but some of us didn't know anyone in the room six months before, and one was there for the first time that day.

Who wouldn't want to be part of a family like that? And if someone didn't want to be, would there be any way to force her to do so that would benefit her and not diminish the value of our time together? I don't think there is. I wouldn't want my kids coming over if they were only doing so because they think I'd be hurt if they didn't. You know you're part of a dysfunctional family if people only attend family functions because they feel obligated to do so.

Turning love into an obligation empties it of reality. Using fear and guilt to get the behavior we want only diminishes love to a pretense. The early believers didn't see fellowship as an obligation. They didn't talk about it as a need with "shoulds," and "musts," and "have tos." They found their life together an endearing reality. They didn't *have* to be together, they *got* to be together.

There are plenty of believers enjoying a relationship with God and deep fellowship without the requisite congregation in the middle of it. They aren't bitter or independent, just more passionate about sharing life relationally than they are about all the meetings and politics they got caught up in when they attended a congregation. And what I've discovered is that those living outside congregational systems don't mind if others feel blessed to be part of them, but those who go to a congregation often judge those who don't.

Unfortunately most Christian groups don't know how to incubate deep and abiding relationships. More often than not the program gets in the way of friendship. The life cycle of any group meeting is usually initial excitement that lasts a few weeks, to people settling in as a habit. Eventually, however, the program becomes routine enough that people start to get bored. People begin to miss, and to keep it alive you have to amp up the program, challenge people to be committed, or find fresh people who will have their own season of excitement. When you go from anticipation to habit, you're not far from actually dreading that day as it rolls around again and looking for excuses to miss.

When that happens we would find it more helpful to ask why it has become routine. Is it because people are losing their spiritual passion or because the gathering no longer supports the passion?

There's never a day I dread my kids or grandkids coming over, or any good friend for that matter. I look forward to any time we gather, savor them when I'm with them, and reflect back on it long after they've left. Real community does that. It's the friendship that takes over and makes it engaging. My first wake-up call to that came when my children were very young and I was still a pastor. At lunch with the local Mennonite minister, I asked him what was the greatest advice he ever received in ministry. Without hesitating he looked up and said, "I know exactly what it was. Someone challenged me not to require my children to attend church after they turned twelve."

I was surprised. I expected something more incisive that helped him teach or counsel people better. But he went on to tell me how much it changed his children. When dad and mom stopped making them go, they had to make some important decisions for themselves. I heard that only a couple of years into helping start a new congregation. My children were four and two at the time. I went home and shared the idea with my wife and we both agreed that it was great counsel and we would follow it. So even though they still had to go with us for a few more years, I wanted to make sure that whatever we did with children would engage them.

I realize some people find this view of the church challenging. They've thought of it only as a meeting to attend and the regular discipline of showing up each week a critical component to their faith. But if that's all it is, it will not stand up to the challenges of life. Large group gatherings can help people learn the basic theology that undergirds a life of faith, but problems arise when it keeps people dependent on the program and doesn't teach them how to live beyond it. If people are not learning how to connect with Jesus and to enjoy growing friendships with others on a similar journey, they will become bored. That's why the program has to continually shift, adding new elements to keep up with the latest fad.

But doesn't Scripture require us to meet together? Most believe it does and quote Hebrews 10:25 as proof. "Let us not give up meeting together, as some are in the habit of doing, but let us encourage one another—and all the more as you see the Day approaching." They apply this to people who no longer feel the need to attend a local congregation because they hunger for more relational expressions of church life, but that isn't the context of this passage. It wasn't written for people who no longer wanted to attend services. It was written for those under persecution who were afraid that their association with other known believers would make it easy for the authorities to identify them and expand the persecution. The writer of Hebrews is assuring them they have more to gain from the encouragement they get from one another than any persecution they would risk.

But notice they gathered to encourage each other, not to sit as spectators at a service. Why do people leave that out and think he's only talking about going to a meeting? Assembling together is more than sitting in a meeting; it means allowing others to walk alongside us as we share mutual encouragement as we follow him. That can happen inside a congregation, but it can also happen outside of it.

Some suggest that Jesus' participation in the synagogue sets an example for believers to meet regularly in a formalized environment. I disagree with the parallel on three points. First, the synagogue was not a large, impersonal, platform-driven event like we hold today. Second, while it was part of Jesus' culture, it predates the new creation and the transformed life it offers. Finally, even those who came out of that culture in the early church did not organize themselves into regular synagogue-like gatherings, but flourished in more spontaneous opportunities for learning, prayer, or fellowship. They initially used the open spaces of the temple for large groups to hear the disciples share their testimony of Jesus' words and actions, and they went to one another's homes to share their newfound joy and to care for one another as needs arose. They gathered to celebrate Peter and John's release from prison and found themselves in prayer for God's boldness in the face of persecution. These were not routine gatherings, but ones that arose as life played out in front of them.

The only other Scripture that talks about church life as a need is in I Corinthians 12. It describes the church as a body and we are all a part of that body. The eye can't say to the hand, *I don't need you,* and separate itself. We are all a piece of a larger whole, and if we live in isolation we're missing out on so much wisdom and strength that come from other people's gifts. One would also be hard-pressed, however, to conclude that this Scripture is a proof text that people need to belong to a congregation to be part of that body. In fact, isn't it those congregations that most often divide us into like-minded groups that deny his work and revelation in others? They cut themselves off from other parts of the body thinking themselves sufficient on their own.

Scripture doesn't teach that everyone needs to be forced into church attendance, but that it would be unwise for you to isolate yourself from the other gifts and insights God has placed around you. People who connect with Jesus will have no inclination to go it alone. God is a community and those who know him will revel in the joy of community with others when it is real.

No matter what expression of the church you engage, if it has become a drudgery you might want to take a fresh look at what you're doing. Programs will produce boredom, but sharing a real connection to God and others never will. Shared life among believers growing to live in his love is inviting, engaging, endearing, attractive, deep, and meaningful. That never gets boring and for that reason is probably the best tool we have to gauge how effective we're sharing life together.

We may have to find our way back to deeper relational engagements, and not by simply adding a "greeting time" to the morning liturgy. Those moments are so superficial as to be meaningless. Friendship happens where people have time to get to know each other and find the safety to be honest about their spiritual hungers and struggles. People being transformed by Jesus through the real challenges they face in life are more engaging than any well-planned service, even when relationships get messy. We are not called just to rejoice with those who rejoice, but also to weep with those who weep. Nothing is more comforting in times of pain than the presence of a close friend who understands and is there to help, and few things are more rewarding than to walk with a friend through a dark place in his or her life.

Friends sharing a journey will also find joy in owning our failures, asking for forgiveness, and looking for ways to iron out conflicts and misunderstandings that demonstrate his love. We're all flawed and will at times disappoint and fail each other, or take offense when none was intended. Friendship, however, allows the kind of honesty that lets us grow in those moments. Were my expectations fair? Was I trespassing on someone else's freedom? Learning to love flawed human beings lies at the heart of learning to be his disciple. If we can't let him love us through our flaws, we won't love others through theirs, and then we won't know how to love those lost in the darkness.

The undercurrent to a life of obligation is the belief that God is not endearing, and life in him is not engaging. Jesus said the purpose of his teaching was so "that my joy may be in you and that your joy may be complete." (John 15:11) Until we see that the life of Jesus is the most engaging invitation we've ever been extended, we won't find our way into its joy. Knowing him will make all he wants for us an irresistible reality. If that's not the case, then you've missed something critical in the gospel.

Everything good does not require a commitment to do what we dislike, but to the simple joy of embracing what we truly love. Obligation presumes that our desires are despicable and lauds those who give up their desires to choose painful tasks for God. But what if your deepest desires are Godly? If he wants your joy to be full then he knows best how to fulfill you. What God identifies as sin are the desires that don't really belong to us. They have been twisted to offer us immediate gratification or false security, while they lead us down a road to certain destruction—spiritually, relationally, and even physically.

You know you've found the life of the church when you find people who genuinely enjoy being together. If relationships are laced with fighting, bickering, and tension, be cautious. Every family has difficult moments, but they are moments—not months of painful, pressure-filled conversations that leave people worn out or devastated at the end. Life's too short and too painful for our faith family to complicate our lives instead of liberating us to know him.

There is nothing more irresistible than exploring your journey alongside others who know how to share God's love and wisdom together. I want to be with them. I want to explore our journeys together, sharing his wisdom and his love for each other. What a joy to watch them be transformed and discover increasing freedom to live in his affection!

Find that conversation with others, and you won't be able to think of the church as a meeting at all, but a gathering of friends.

14 | Gatherings without Meetings

... let us encourage one another—and all the
more as you see the Day approaching.

HEBREWS 10:25

Characteristic Four:
The depth of relationship is valued over pre-planned meetings.

"**I**f meetings could usher in the kingdom of God we would have done it by now."

Those words came out of the mouth of John Beaumont as he sat across from me in his home in Rotorua, New Zealand. In my preparations to write this book, I traveled all over the world in what I affectionately called my "Old Coot Tour" talking with those in their seventies and eighties who have explored more relational ways of church life. As an author, pastor, and speaker, John, then just shy of his eightieth birthday, had traveled the world attending and conducting thousands upon thousands of meetings with a passion to help others experience a vibrant life in Christ. Yet he had come to recognize that the energy put into planning and holding meetings had a negligible effect on advancing the kingdom of God. I was in stitches as he hilariously ranted about all the fruitless time he had spent not only in meetings but also in what he called "meetings about meetings." He said real fellowship always ends when meetings begin and returns when they end. Through the laughter, his point was made. The new creation thrives in relationships not in meetings.

His comments crystallized something I'd been noticing for some time. As much as I enjoy standing up front and talking to a large group of people, it is not the most effective environment to pass on the life of the kingdom. I find myself far more attracted to the conversations that go on before and after a meeting. I've held all-day workshops with rooms full of people and though they can be helpful, it's the following day I enjoy most. I usually hang out in someone's home while a constant stream of people flow through, which allows an opportunity for people to ask the difficult questions and recognize God's hand in their own lives. On the first day we talk mostly about issues and concepts; on the second we talk about life and people finding their way into it. On the first day people are guarded in a public venue; on the second they're freer to talk about themselves and their struggles.

Is this why Jesus never called a meeting? Even when he was in the upper room celebrating their first communion, he was in a conversation with the disciples, not guiding them through a liturgy or agenda.

Though healthy families get together often, they rarely have meetings or lectures. They have conversations around a table, a campfire, or a leisurely afternoon on the patio. We gather when tragedy strikes or for celebrations of joy, but never to have a meeting. Can you imagine if my children showed up for Christmas dinner and instead of place settings around the table I seated them in rows with an order of service laying on each chair? It would be laughable because the reality of family life would give way to the contrived.

That's not to suggest meetings are evil. If my family ran a business or a foundation together, we would have meetings that the task demands, but they wouldn't define our relationship. There are many reasons to meet with other believers—to share information, to work on a project, or to organize an event. But these would be for a specific time and purpose, not the routine of our life together. Relationships grow at gatherings, not meetings.

What's the difference? Am I just splitting semantic hairs here? I realize the terms can be used synonymously, but I'm not doing so. A *gathering* brings people together to celebrate relationship. It is heavy on conversation, often multiple conversations, because people are not forced to follow an agenda. *Meetings,* on the other hand, bring people together to accomplish a task, even if that task is to perform some ritual. They demand conformity and people have to cooperate for them to work. Relationships are not critical, which is why you can attend meetings for years, even small ones, and not get to know or care for others in the group.

Meetings have a limited shelf life once they've accomplished their task. Beyond that they simply self-perpetuate by obligating people to attend and often become a place to hide from real human engagements. That's why people will prefer 24/7 prayer/worship gatherings when they haven't even learned to love their spouse, their kids, or their neighbors.

The signal of church life is not easily found in large meetings of like-minded people, but in the engagements of growing friendships. Success is measured not by the size of the group but by the quality of relationships. Instead of complicating people's time with meetings and commitments, real church life is more readily experienced with authentic friendships in informal settings that don't require large resources to drive centralized programs.

You can't share life with hundreds of people sitting in a managed group. You can share a cause, a task even, but relationships won't grow for the lack of time and energy to explore them. Isn't that why people feel so disconnected in large congregations and complain that the relationships they do have remain superficial?

Recently I met Ronel when a group of us got together to talk about our passions for his church. Her story is not so different from many I hear who transition from meeting-focused to being grounded relationally:

I have to say my time with you was divine intervention. (It) opened my eyes to something I was not expecting. I went having recently decided to step down from women's ministry at a mega-church because I was constantly having a carrot of freedom dangled in front of me but it was laced with control and conformity. I just knew it was not where I belonged. Prior to attending the meeting I had discussed house church and some other new ideas with my husband. (But) seeing all those people struggling with control issues in house church was an eye opener to the reality that man-made religious groups with rules will lead to frustration.

I left that meeting with a sense of peace about not attending "church" and exploring life with Father. Honestly it felt a little lonely at first but as the weeks wore on I realized that I had a phone full of numbers and the ability to invite couples over for dinner or girlfriends out to coffee. As long as Father was with me he was in the conversation. This awakening to the realization that I need to make connection a priority instead of having it manufactured for me in a building was vital to my soul. I am taking this journey one day at a time but honestly I could not imagine a more beautiful picture of our family learning to navigate this together. Whether we are on the wrestling mats with our son, in the dugout at little league, or all curled up on the bed reading a book, I am seeing with new eyes that all my busyness was stealing these precious moments.

Jesus moved Ronel and her family from thinking about church as a meeting she had to find or create, to instead walk alongside people she already knew. This is where his church incubates. I know this scares people who would rather Ronel and her husband invest their gifts and talents in their organization, or at the very least host a meeting that others could attend, but that would only prolong their struggle. Jesus is opening a wider door for them, not of fitting themselves into conformity-based systems, but exploring how his church takes expression in the relationships around them.

Even if you are part of a more traditional congregation, it will help you to think relationally about your engagement with it. It's not going to be enough to sit in a meeting with people; you'll want to connect with them at a deeper level. As some say, not so tongue-in-cheek, the life of the church is better expressed as people go in and out of the parking lot, than in our services.

When I was a pastor I was afraid that if people weren't committed to meetings they would end up one of those lone-ranger Christians who just worry about themselves and end up isolated. Looking back, I was probably only trying to protect my turf. Now I know that as people grow closer to Jesus, love will draw them into community. They find less relevance in preprogrammed meetings and more desire for relationships they couldn't find when everyone was so busy with the program. What Ronel and her husband will discover is how church makes itself known out of those relational engagements. Yes, it takes some initiative. No one is planning meetings to give you the illusion of fellowship. You'll need to sort through your own relationships and find those with whom God is inviting you to engage more intentionally. It will take time for those friendships to deepen and for people to be interconnected, but the gatherings that grow out of relationships are far more engaging than any meeting we devise.

No, we cannot have a deep, personal friendship with everyone we meet. But we can give time and attention to those Jesus invites us into and by that share his life with them. You'll soon discover that you'll have different spheres of relationships, which is entirely appropriate. On the outer edges are people you're just getting to know. Conversations tend to be a bit more awkward here because you don't have the details of their lives and still aren't sure where their personal boundaries lie, but if you let them grow through the awkwardness you never know what will happen down the road. Every close friend you have today was a stranger at one point.

Some of those acquaintances actually become friends, people you seek out because you find them an encouragement in your own journey or because you want to encourage them. It may begin just because you have a sense that God has a connection there for you. Time and proximity may not allow you to be together regularly, but when you do you come away grateful to be in their lives.

Some of these will become closer friends. At any one time we may have two or three dozen people who are in touch with us regularly. They may not have all the details, but they certainly grasp the big picture. We may share regular gatherings with some of these, work on a project together, or simply connect more intentionally. These conversations can go deep rather quickly because of the safety and concern we have for the other.

The smallest sphere are those intimate friends with whom we cross paths multiple times during the week and whom we know well enough to speak with honestly and caringly. We are inside each other's journeys as an encouragement on a regular basis. You are a blessed person if you have even two or three of these at any one time, and you probably won't have time for more than half a dozen at one time.

As relationships deepen, your mutual passion for Jesus and his kingdom will deepen as well. You may even know people you treasure who don't yet know the God you know, but what better way for them to meet him than through your love for them? Of course these are only rough guidelines and we will want to be careful not to put a fine-line definition on our relationships. Relational life is incredibly fluid and if we try to pin it down or organize it with too many details, it will be like sticking a butterfly to a Styrofoam collection. Once you do, it ceases to be a butterfly. These are not hard and fast ideas, but I want to give some idea of the ebb and flow of friendships. Please don't make a chart for your refrigerator so you can classify everyone you know into one of these spheres. People will move in and out of them in various seasons due to need, proximity, and interest. Some may be around for a significant season, others for a lifetime.

Yes, that means at any one time you'll have a closer relationship with some than others. Some people may see this as a clique, but it's not unless it becomes exclusive. Relationships grounded in the new creation are always open—I see value in blessing others with the same friendships that have been a blessing to me. I find it impossible to manage this on my own, but I am growing to trust Jesus to show me who fits into my life at any given season and what new people he wants me to invest in. Learn to flow with his Spirit as he nudges you rather than trying to control it yourself.

A few years ago God connected me with a group of believers who live south of Dublin in Ireland. More than forty years ago, they were a group of evangelicals who had experienced a fresh awakening of the Spirit that was transforming their lives. They expanded in the '70s as the Charismatic movement took hold of the Catholic Church in Ireland, and they took on more characteristics of an organized house church. By the mid-'80s, their weekly meetings had lost their freshness and monotony began to creep in. One cold winter when the heating broke in the hall where they met, they decided to meet informally in a few homes. Immediately their fellowship freshened again.

After further prayer, they concluded God was asking them to lay down their weekly meeting and their appointed leadership. In the future, they would only meet together whenever he gave them a specific purpose to do so. Other than that, they encouraged everyone to listen to the Lord as to how they would continue to be together. For the next thirty years, they lived as a community in and out of one another's homes, praying and listening to God together, helping each other as any had need. They grew in Christ, vacationed together, presented a musical for their community, learned about God, and shared their relationships with any who came along. They found themselves connected to people in distant countries, and they often traveled to share in those relationships, as well as hosted when others visited.

Because they didn't create an institution that they had to manage, they have continued as great friends. They've never had a broken relationship even if some felt the desire to attend a traditional congregation. Their gatherings are more like a holiday or family reunion than a Sunday service, and yet people have been loved, discipled, equipped, transformed, and drawn into an authentic life of faith and community.

Gatherings can be so much more effective because everyone is not forced into the same activity at the same time. There's a flow to their life together that is determined by the breath of the Spirit, and what's going on in each other's lives. By not creating artificial environments that others have to fit in to, their life together rises out of what God is doing in each of them. Instead of hearing sermons, whose topic may not fit into their current journey, they are talking about their struggles and getting help where it's more needful.

One group I know in South Africa periodically takes a hike together on Sunday morning before reconvening at a picnic area to cook breakfast together. Since I was their guest that morning, I started with the first group out and during the course of our one and a half hour hike made my way back through the entire group having a variety of conversations that I let others initiate. People got to talk about what helped them most, not what I might have shared in a sermon. I find the best teaching unfolds in a conversation with a hungry heart and an observation or question that opens their heart to God's work in them—exactly what Jesus did for a woman at a well or the disciples fighting over who would be first in the kingdom.

That walk in the woods is a great metaphor for the ebb and flow of relational community among a group of people during months and years. As we'll see in subsequent chapters, in that space there is room for teaching, elders to be known, collaborations to occur, and people to be cared for. Everything Scripture offers about the church has a fulfillment in relational life and gatherings. That's why we know far more about how the early church loved, struggled, taught, admonished, served, encouraged, and submitted to one another, than anything about how to conduct a preplanned meeting.

And once you discover just how amazing it is to grow friendships and find connections, you'll always wonder how you thought the life of the church could ever find expression in a regimented meeting.

15 | Authority without Hierarchy

> Sheep, taking turns pretending to be the shepherd.
>
> PSALM 53:3 (MSG)

Characteristic Five:
Authority rises from the revelation of Jesus, not from well-crafted structures.

Yes, I know it seems unthinkable. How can authority exist without hierarchy?

All of society is organized by hierarchical systems, be it government, business, or even a local service club. You can't organize a group without clarifying the chain of command and who has the authority to make decisions. It is the water we swim in, so it doesn't surprise me when our forbearers of faith tried to organize the church into institutions that would also fall into the hierarchy trap.

It certainly didn't start that way. Jesus didn't give them that plan and the early apostles demonstrated no tendency to adopt this old creation system to manage the life of the church. It seems to me that as the vibrancy of first-century faith in Jesus to be the practical head of his church waned over time, the early believers retreated back to the only system they knew—an established hierarchy to determine who had the authority to make decisions, approve theology, and set the rules and rituals the faithful had to follow. We have tried thousands of such systems during the past two thousand years and none proved effective at sustaining a vitality of church life or bringing the church to unity. Having a multiplicity of hierarchies that claim to speak for Christ has fragmented the church, confused its proclamation of the Gospel, and emptied it of its power by reducing it to just another human institution.

Those who reach the top echelons of leadership have rarely resisted the temptations of power that lead to the same arrogance, political infighting, and competition for cash, credit, and control that mars the old creation. Followers are taught to respect the process even if they disagree with the results and to trust that God works through such leadership no matter how flawed they are. While Scripture teaches us to respect government officials and trust God's hand behind history even if they don't acknowledge him, it makes no such claim for those who set themselves up in leadership positions for "the church."

A cursory view of history makes it clear that a hierarchy of human leadership does more to disfigure the church than it does to protect it. Perhaps the severest price we've paid for doing so is that we no longer see authority resting in Jesus but in the institutions we have created by our own hand—perhaps not so dissimilar from the idols crafted in ancient Israel to replace the God they could not see.

I've talked to many a young "church planter" describing their vision to create a new group that will be truer to Scripture, more relational, and better at helping people follow Jesus than those who have come before. They think no one has planted a church with that vision when almost all of them have only ended up weighted down with a structure that cannot sustain it. Instead of rethinking the validity of the system, they assume it is flawed because the wrong people are in charge. Once the white hats take over, all will be well. They don't realize it is the system of management itself that passes out the black hats.

None of us are immune from the deception of privilege and power and how they can distort our perspective when we have to act for the good of an institution, rather than yielding to the breath of the Spirit. The only way to control people is to enact a system of rewards and punishments, no matter how benign. Soon wealth and power gather at the peak of the pyramid and it becomes top-heavy, exploiting people rather than serving them. All human systems do it, especially those that claim to follow God. Even if they co-opt the language of servant leadership, the ruse is unmasked by the simple fact that money and benefits flow upward and control downward.

We need look no further than the Pharisees to find a group of leaders who took God's words and twisted them into a platform for their own prestige and power. As people come to live in the reality of the new creation, however, any hierarchy begins to feel like a straitjacket. Jesus never intended for the life of the new creation to fit into structures of the old. He didn't start an organization and install himself as CEO. He said that the greatest in his kingdom would find serving more vital than command. He didn't tell people what to do, but invited them into a kingdom in which love would negate the need for control.

And yet, the one thing that astounded people around him was the authority by which he spoke. Jesus did not hold any academic degrees, civic or religious positions of authority, nor did he claim to be rabbi or prophet in any formal sense. His authority was derived from three complementary sources. First, his words were not the convoluted language of religious spin-doctors, but expressed the core realities of the universe and resonated when people heard them. Second, those words were backed by the power of an indestructible life. His words resounded with the authenticity of someone who truly believed them and lived them. Finally, he genuinely cared about people, seeking to serve them not to exploit them, and that, too, was obvious.

Jesus' example separated authority from hierarchy. The early apostles seemed to have gotten the message and did nothing to create a centralized structure in Jerusalem to manage the burgeoning church. In the litany of human history that is so unique as to be profound. While some argue that the council at Jerusalem (Acts 15) was proof that the Apostles ruled over the congregations, a reading of Acts comes to a very different conclusion. All the brothers were together and they were seeking a solution for the good of all. The apostles offered no edict that everyone had to follow. James offered an assessment that resonated with others present so that they could say that it "seemed good to them and to the Holy Spirit." What's more, they didn't use the occasion to set up an institutional hierarchy, define orthodoxy by doctrinal statements, or write a long list of regulations for the church to follow. They asked only three things—abstain from immorality, remember the poor, and don't eat meat offered to idols. Can you imagine any group today that would come up with such a simple solution to not burdening others or setting up a permanent council to resolve future conflicts?

Their instructions were as minimalist as possible, and even one of those was eventually undermined when Paul recognized that abstaining from meat offered to idols was more in deference to Jewish sentiment than grounded in truth. When Paul later concluded that people were free to eat meat sacrificed to idols, he even made room for people to disagree with his view. He encouraged them to live to their own conscience, not his. (1 Corinthians 8) If they thought false gods were real enough to taint food, he would honor their conscience. He did not need to command obedience because he was building them up to be sensitive to the Spirit's guidance.

As long as we see authority tethered to hierarchical systems and the power to manage people, we will miss real authority and the opportunity to embrace it.

Real authority resides in Jesus.

When Jesus ascended the Father gave all authority to him. Anyone demonstrates that authority only as his or her words, actions, and demeanor align with God's reality, character, and purpose. James carried the day in Jerusalem, not because he held a position that God honored, but because others recognized Jesus in what he shared. Jesus seemed content to let people recognize truth when they heard it. If we give that designation away to our institutional processes we have embraced an allegiance that will confuse our fidelity to Christ. When we base authority on anything other than an embodiment of God's truth, be it by title, position, employment, academic degree, or alleged apostolic succession, we take a step away from helping people learn to follow Jesus and substitute someone or some thing in his place.

But doesn't that mean everyone is free to do what's right in his or her own eyes? Yes, that is the essence of our freedom in Christ; otherwise we're no different than Israel rejecting God's leadership by asking to have a king like all the other nations. What if people make mistakes? They will, but by reaping the benefits of truth where we see it and facing the consequences where we miss it, we'll sharpen our senses to discern truth from error. Add to the fact that no one commands a large, centralized system, failures are relatively contained and don't have a widespread impact.

I trust good-hearted people listening to Jesus more than I trust any hierarchy whose perspective is so easily skewed by the needs of their institution or the realities that let them hold on to power. The historic heresies have not arisen from simple people following Jesus, but from someone trying to gain a large following. In my experience, those who live this way don't become fiercely independent and are easily seduced into error. On the contrary, they seek out others that will help them identify the truth Jesus has placed in their hearts.

Real authority illuminates Truth.

Knowledge is a valuable tool. To understand the basics of

theology, Scripture's story of redemption and the nature of God and his purpose in us will be of great help to you as you learn to embrace the new creation. If you're new to this journey, seek out some good instruction along these lines. However, Paul warned us that, "Knowledge puffs up, but love builds up." (I Corinthians 8:1) Theology without transformation only leads to arrogance.

His authority blends truth and love and makes itself evident in an observation, question, or action that illuminates a truth God has already put in someone's heart. I guess you could say that authority is truth in action and opens a door for someone to respond to the reality of the new creation already at work in the heart. That's why Paul, even as an apostle, refused to resort to manipulative tactics. On the contrary he said ". . . by setting forth the truth plainly we commend ourselves to every man's conscience in the sight of God." (2 Corinthians 4:2)

Authority has a power beyond knowledge. Those who have it are not defensive or argumentative because they know truth carries its own power when people are ready. And if they are not ready, pushing them will not be helpful. Authority looks for the opening that allows light to shine into the darkness. It realizes truth is not fragile and will always win in the end where opinions won't count, lies will unravel, and false teaching will fail. Only truth will endure.

Real authority is not the power to command.

Authority in the old creation is always about control—who gets to lead and who has to follow. How many have taught Paul's call to submission in marriage as a contest of power? The husband is in charge so the wife must submit. That wasn't Paul's point at all. In the new creation submission is not about power or privilege, reducing the wife to a second-class citizen. Her submission is to the husband's responsibility to ensure that his wife gets to be all Jesus wants her to be. Authority is a place to serve and support, not command.

That's why people who understand the nature of real authority gravitate away from boards and committees that waste the time and energy of gifted lives to manage people. Instead of loving people into wholeness, they are cajoling them into following the rules. If you think you are responsible for making others conform to God's standards, where do you stop when they resist? Today we punish them with gossip, shaming, and excluding, but in times past it included torture and execution. Even some of our revered reformers used threats and violence to force people to capitulate to their view of God's will.

We create most of our human systems, be they organizational or philosophical, in hopes of protecting people from that chaos of human experience. But no system has been able to do that, so we endlessly tweak it in hopes of finding just the right balance. Have you noticed God demonstrates no such passion to manage the chaos? His authority moves in the midst of chaos to unfold his kingdom and invite people into the new creation. I find greater joy in expressing his presence in the midst of chaos, rather than fruitlessly trying to devise a system that will keep it at bay.

If authority is not derived from being in charge of a group, no one has to decide who belongs to Christ and who doesn't. The church is built on this one foundation: God knows those who are his. (2 Timothy 2:19) If he does, we don't have to. That's why Jesus warned his disciples not to try to separate the wheat from weeds or they would end up destroying both. The authority of the new creation is an invitation to life, a carrot not a stick. If people don't want to come you have no authority to make them do so.

Real authority is recognized not demanded.

Perhaps the funniest phone call I ever received was from a father in the throes of anguish from an ongoing battle between him and his wife and daughters over an issue that was tearing at the fabric of their home. He was so sure he was right and dismissive of their point of view. I could tell he was angry as soon as I answered the phone. His voice was high-pitched and frantic, "Wayne, just tell me when I'm going to get the respect from my wife and children I deserve?"

I barely hit the mute button before I exploded into laughter.

Fortunately he raged on for twenty minutes, giving me time to compose myself. This was a friend of mine, so I didn't think his crisis was funny. Far from it! He was in great pain. It was just that his question sounded so absurd. When I asked him what he was saying to his wife and kids by calling his conclusion a "no brainer," he went silent. After a few moments his eyes opened to see that the disrespect he was getting was the same as he was giving.

If you have to demand authority, you don't have it. You can tell someone has no understanding of God's authority when they take on a deeper, more authoritative voice, or grow more agitated or sullen when people disagree with them. Christ's voice needs no such embellishment. The truest words I have ever heard weren't shouted from a pulpit, but spoken plainly in simple conversation with people who knew something about Jesus that I needed to hear.

Real authority establishes the kingdom.

The authority of the church was never to manage our institutions or preserve sound doctrine, but to co-labor alongside Jesus as his prayer is answered: "Your kingdom come, your will be done on earth as it is in heaven." As powerful as community is between brothers and sisters and as much as he wants us to delight in growing, healthy relationships that share his life together, the fruit of that community is to extend the effective range of God's will by walking alongside him in prayer and declaration of the power of the kingdom.

The keys Jesus referred to when he affirmed Peter's confession as the rock on which the church would be built (Matthew 16) extend God's dominion over the world. This invites us into a spiritual dimension that too often remains a mystery. It doesn't mean we get to use God to control events or to make other people do his bidding. This authority joins the Father in his work; it doesn't enlist him in ours. Through prayer and obedience to him, we can extend the boundaries of his kingdom in the domains where we live. We'll revisit this in more detail when we talk about the unity of the church out of which this kind of authority grows exponentially.

By defining the nature of his authority, I am not advancing ignoring authority structures in the old. Governments are obvious, unless they demand that we defy God in deference to them. There are authority structures where you work and almost any group you join. There's an authority to someone else's presence, respecting them and making room for their conscience. These structures serve a purpose in preserving society when people don't see eye to eye. God respects such things, which is why he does not force anyone to love him.

Walking in Christ's authority will allow you to be in a variety of environments without forcing your will on others. When we are in the orbit of some institutional authority, love would call us to respect it, even if we disagree with it. When I speak in a congregation, I never overstep the invitation I've been given without explicit nudging from God. I can encourage God's work among them in the space I've been given. If you attend a congregation, respect the structures that govern their life together. When you can't, then it is time to leave. You can do so quietly without a defiant last stand or disaffecting others.

When I work with others on a project we set up clear decision-making processes so we won't be paralyzed by inaction when we're not in agreement. I will fight long for unanimous heart-felt agreement, but not every decision allows the time or energy for that so we always have someone "on point" to make decisions when we don't agree. Of course, just because someone gets to make the decision doesn't mean they'll make the right one. Time will tell, which is why it is best to keep whatever structures we use to a minimum and keep them temporary.

For those who, as we come to the end of this chapter, are worried that removing our hierarchical systems will only create anarchy, I have great news for you. Where Jesus is the Head our freedom from the control of others won't devolve into chaos—it opens a door for a different kind of order that only love can produce.

16 | Order without Control

Honor one another above yourselves.
ROMANS 12:10

Characteristic Six:
Order comes from mutual respect and affection, not from policies and rules.

"What's wrong with you and Julie?" The bite in my wife's words startled me as we watched our daughter and her children pull out of our driveway.

I turned with an inquisitive look. "And, what are we talking about?"

"Why do you two make rules in my garden?"

Uh oh!

Our granddaughters had just spent the day with us and a lot of that had been in Sara's English garden, which is a sight to behold! She spends countless hours creating this paradise. A rose-covered archway greets you as you enter and wood-chipped pathways meander among a vast array of flowers. Sara had purchased plastic rakes for the girls and when I saw one of them raking the wood chips into piles I explained how she was doing it wrong and how to rake out the wood chips evenly. Her eyes turned sad and within seconds, she had lost interest in the rake. Later, when my daughter arrived she saw her children picking flowers and told them to stop. "You have to ask Grandma before you pick her flowers."

We both thought we were helping, of course, but explaining that to Sara didn't work. She held my arm, looked into my eyes, and smiled. "There's nothing my grandkids can do in that garden that I can't fix in ten minutes after they've gone. I don't care how many flowers they pick; that's why I grow them. The only thing I want is for them to enjoy being in my garden." I got the message. Who wants to be a killjoy in the garden anyway? I was only doing it for her, and if she didn't want it, so much the better.

But in her words I heard a bigger voice in a greater garden. How often have I made rules in God's garden that destroyed the joy of his children growing up there? By using systems of control to protect his church, we unwittingly suck all the joy out of it. People who have only known "church" in that environment cannot envision a society without human leadership to maintain order and communication. What they have not considered, and perhaps have never had the opportunity to see, is what happens when a network of people live under the Shepherd's direction. They do not need those systems, and in fact find them a distraction. As people learn to live free of the dominance of their flesh, why would they need safeguards designed for an old creation? Institutions need control to function; people need love to grow.

The church of Jesus flourishes where people respect one another with love and honor, preferring the needs of others above their own and leaving the management to the Head. It is his body and when we take control on his behalf, it is the surest sign we don't believe in his capability to build it himself. We have demonstrated that throughout "church" history. Perhaps the best example of it in my lifetime was the Shepherding Movement of the late '70s and early '80s.

As the Charismatic renewal grew, people engaged a more active God than some of the denominations would allow. Many people left their congregations to form new ones or house churches, but encountering problems and lack of a larger identity they appealed to a group of influential teachers based in Florida. They had found the joy of fellowship and collaboration in a relational fellowship with one another and had formalized that relationship into a covenant that became a model for others. Unfortunately, that proved to be a fateful step down an institutional road.

Desiring to help others and provide protection for them, but as yet unaware of the limitations of human systems to manage the church, they constructed a hierarchy of leadership that began in Ft. Lauderdale. Through various levels, they reached localities all over the world to manage the groups that had grown in their wake. As in all human-designed systems, control moved downward and money moved upward. The local level tithed to their leader, who tithed to the leader above them and so on, essentially creating a multi-level marketing scheme ripe for corruption. And it soon followed, not only in financial misuse, but also in oppressive authority. What began as wiser men trying to help others, soon became insecure leaders enforcing their authority by demanding unquestioned obedience. It grew so dark that even the organizers themselves had to repudiate their own system.

What went wrong? By serving the cry of their followers to provide leadership, they discovered once again humanity's inability to resist the lusts of cash, credit, and control.

Instead of using their gifts to equip others to trust and follow him, they gave in to the temptation to build their own version of it. I have met people all over the world who were exploited and abused in that movement. Fortunately many of them have found the grace to move past the mistakes of those days and have grown in their ever-maturing dependence on Jesus. They no longer look to human systems to manage what only Jesus can control. One survivor, Tom Mohn, talks with great passion now about a church he knows that is "rooted outside of history" with "no visible means of support" and yet alive with Christ's power. He goes on to say, "The moment we view the church as an institution and part of the world's system she has lost her virginity and her power," and "to equate the church with a flow chart is a sacrilege, at least, and demonic, at worst."

Are people like him jaded because of hurt, or were their eyes opened through it to find the beauty of a church that is untainted by human management? During the past twenty years I've come to appreciate a church that functions with unmediated spirituality, unmanaged community, and unmaintained networks that span the world. Growing trust in him allows us to let go of our need to be in control and simply participate with him as his glory unfolds.

Unmediated spirituality means that we all have direct access to God through the work of the Son. There is only one mediator between God and man, and it is the man Christ Jesus. (I Timothy 2:5) No one who understands that would insert themselves between Jesus and his people, and no one understanding it would look for a leader to follow instead of Jesus himself. The invitation of the New Covenant is that "all will know me, from the least of them to the greatest." (Hebrews 8:11) There may be others further down the road than you are, and they can be incredibly helpful in equipping you to know God and learn what it means for you to follow him. But those who follow Jesus will never ask you to follow them or their program instead.

Unmanaged community means we don't substitute the regularity of a group for the community that grows out of friendship. Instead of filling our lives with meetings and caretaking institutions, we get to spend time inviting people into our lives, engaging in relationships with them as he directs, and enjoying the fruit of those friendships. Community is found in relationships of affection, the sharing of his life, and the freedom to do whatever he asks of us.

Unmaintained networks are the wider connections the Spirit gives us across cities, states, and countries. I have been amazed at the way he knits hearts together around the world as people are generous with their friendships. While not all are inclined to travel, everyone I know locally benefits by the friendships I have in other countries. Their conversations and discoveries get seeded into ours, and ours into theirs. Through those relationships wisdom spreads, our view of God broadens, and resources combine to accomplish countless tasks.

I realize how scary it can be to move away from our program-based activities and actually think that building relationships with others will let the church take expression among us. It does run counter to everything we've been taught. I've watched it happen over years, however, and I've never found more breathtaking and powerful examples of church life than when we are no longer in charge and catch a flow of the Spirit that weaves his wonder into our lives.

A few years ago some of my friends in Ireland invited people learning to live in Father's affection from all over the world to come to County Wicklow for a weeklong gathering. They asked me to come and to invite any others I thought it might bless. I invited a number of people, but one man from Africa had a hard time understanding what exactly we were doing. Is it a conference? No, it's just a gathering of people. Will there be meetings? No, we're just going to be together and see what God does. Will you be giving any teachings? Not in any formal sense.

He wasn't sure it was going to be worth his time, and I understood that. He was leaving job and family and purchasing a costly ticket to come to something he couldn't define. More than a hundred people were going to be together for a week. The only organized events included a potluck on the first Sunday, a bus tour of the surrounding countryside on Monday, and a barbecue on the final Saturday. He struggled with it for weeks since it felt more like a holiday than something spiritually significant. I didn't press him; it was just an invitation.

In the end he came, and I stood with him at the corner of a large tent staked in a field as the barbecue was concluding. My friend was euphoric. He said he'd never had a week like that and he was so spiritually enriched from the people he met. "I cannot believe what has happened in these six days. I've heard more teaching, been prayed for, shared some insights with others, heard more prophecy than anything I'd ever been a part of in my life."

When people who are on a spiritual journey get near each other, the church takes expression. He had no idea what simple joy and life could come out of being together and how fruitful it would be, not only for that week but also for years to come because of the new friendships that were formed. I've had the joy of watching a web of relationships grow around the world and see how those connections enrich Christ's work and allow us to see him more fully.

For that to continue, however, we all have to resist the temptation to throw a structure around it and start monthly, quarterly, or yearly meetings. By doing so we sow the seeds for a new faction in the family and seriously damage the spontaneity of his work by putting a human agenda to it. As excited as I was to be part of this Wicklow gathering a few years ago, I was thrilled that at its end no one pressed to make it a yearly event or formalize a network. There have been other gatherings in other places as people felt inspired to plan and host them, but there has been no attempt to get the same people together at the same place. In fact many on this journey have a hesitation to repeat anything only because it was wonderful the first time, given our propensity to value routine over reality. Tradition is the attempt to get God to repeat something he did once, again and again to the same results. But the breath of the Spirit is too unique for such attempts and we only end up capturing ourselves in routines long after he has moved on.

The point in all of this is not that we live unmediated, unmanaged, and unmaintained lives; it's just that we're trusting Jesus to do the mediating, the managing, and the maintaining. There's no way our traditions and programs can ever capture that same reality.

A few months ago a local pastor whom I'd never met was prevailed upon to give me a manuscript as a favor to a friend. He called, somewhat tentatively, to ask if he could drop it by. That exchange turned into a two-hour conversation. A few days later he invited me to lunch and we were once again stirred by the thoughts and passions of the other. A couple of months later I woke up with him on my heart, so we set up another lunch. At the end of it he suggested we start getting together every month. Just the thought turned my stomach a bit, not because I wouldn't want to be with him, but I knew the growing friendship would change if we turned it into a regular meeting instead of trusting Jesus to bring us together when next it pleases him.

I offered him a different option. "Why don't we continue just like we have? When I'm next on your heart, contact me, and when you are on mine, I'll contact you?" I know that sounds flaky to some, but try it for six months and you'll discover that the conversations that rise out of the wind of the Spirit are a hundred times more fruitful than those of routine and habit. Now we get together when we want to and have something to talk about instead of trying to figure out what to talk about because we are getting together.

What prevents these more relational engagements from becoming chaotic? As I've watched them happen during the last twenty years, I'm reminded of two Scriptures that give us the wisdom to let order rise relationally rather than be imposed from without.

"Be devoted to one another in brotherly love. Honor one another above yourselves." (Romans 12:10) Paul invited the Romans to put relationships of love above any other consideration. When we value the friendship enough we will honor each other even above our own desires. Managed groups have to restrain the indulgent and immature so they can't exploit the environment. You won't exploit people you care about and you will bend over backward to ensure that all are cared for rather than scheming to get your own way.

"Speaking the truth in love, we will in all things grow up into him who is the Head, that is, Christ." (Ephesians 4:15) When people share relationships that are open and honest, deeply grounded in their affection for each other, everything that needs to come to light does. Nothing will destroy this process faster than selfishness, divisiveness, deceit, gossip, or betrayal. Where they do arise people can be lovingly confronted and invited into greater freedom so they won't be destructive. Affection-based honesty is all the protection a group needs. Problems can be resolved with such graciousness that people either want to change or they will withdraw realizing they don't fit in. It provides healthy boundaries as no one is forced to go beyond their freedom.

Where these realities converge, generosity and humility become the powerful mixture that will referee our life together by maintaining order without having to put people under control. People can have vastly different perspectives and still respect each other while they seek wisdom that integrates both concerns instead of fighting for their own. Where we come to know his wisdom together the possibilities are limitless. Where people cannot share lovingly, the expression of the church among them wanes, as well it should without leaving a dead institution behind.

Where generosity and humility flourish, the church becomes more visible. It opens the door to some amazing collaborations in helping others or fulfilling some other project more easily, at less expense, and without the overhead of a permanent ministry.

Where a culture of mutual honor and respect define how people share life together, it opens the door to a oneness of heart and purpose that will transform the world.

17 Unity without Conformity

You have only one Master and you are all brothers.

MATTHEW 23:8

Characteristic Seven:
Unity emerges from wholehearted agreement,
not from conformity imposed from outside.

The best moments in my nearly forty-year marriage to Sara are those when we are doing something together that we both wholeheartedly enjoy and are both fully invested in. No, we don't live like that all the time. Not all our interests overlap so we don't do everything together. Some days we're sorting through conflicts or differences of opinion. Sometimes I'll give up what I would prefer to serve her. Other times she lays down her life to participate in something with me. Those days are special, too, because love runs deep when it does not seek its own.

But in those moments when our desires, insights, and passions overlap completely and with one heart and mind, and we are engaged together, we get to celebrate the fullness of what it means to be not two people, but one in agreement and joy. That can happen in a project around the house, making an important decision, giving our lives away to someone who needs help, a moment of recreation, spending an evening with friends we both love, or even in celebrating the intimacy of our marriage.

The Psalmist knew that joy as he exclaimed how good and pleasant it is when God's people live in unity! (Psalm 33) There is really nothing like it! Finding your way into the genuine affection, humility, and generosity that lets you experience this depth of unity with your spouse makes every day a joyful adventure. Although marriage is prime real estate to discover how mutual selflessness leads to oneness, it is certainly not the only one. Paul invited the young church on a similar adventure: "Make every effort to keep the unity of the Spirit in the bond of peace, and to be of one mind." (Ephesians 4:2)

We've been leading up to this chapter since the book began. The power of the church lies in the unity they find together—men and women loving and working together wholeheartedly because they have found their life and joy in him instead of their own preferences and ideas. How could any conformity-based system produce this unity when people are following the expectations of others rather than living out of an ever-expanding heart? Without that, real unity cannot exist.

Early on I was part of a church that was of one mind because only one mind was allowed to function—the senior pastor's. Everyone else had to shut up and go along. If you couldn't follow his every whim, then you needed to leave. Some of the so-called revival movements talk openly about people "supporting the vision of the house" by unquestioned obedience to the man at the top. Institutions need that kind of conformity for an aggressive program, but any unity it produces is artificial, contrived, and short-lived.

Jesus prayed for a very different process:

> I pray also for those who will believe in me through their message, that all of them may be one, Father, just as you are in me and I am in you. May they also be in us so that the world may believe that you have sent me. I have given

them the glory that you gave me, that they may be one as we are one—I in them and you in me—so that they may be brought to complete unity. Then the world will know that you sent me and have loved them even as you have loved me. (John 17:20–23)

Let the majesty of those words sink in. Jesus didn't pray for conformity, but a unity that can only arise out of lives transformed by his glory. The answer to this prayer fulfills God's passion in the earth and by it the world will know that the Father loves us as much as he loves his Jesus. When people out of diverse backgrounds come to complete unity of heart, purpose, and focus, God is unveiled in a way nothing else can accomplish.

Of course this is the Father's to do. It would be impossible for humanity to produce anything close to it, which is why Jesus asks his Father to give it, not his disciples to work on it. I've tasted it many times in my life. When I get to know people from other cultures and we can almost complete each other's sentences when we talk about him, then I know how powerful this unity is. It's not because we've read the same books or memorized the same catechism, but because we are coming to know the same Father and learning to trust him enough to lose our own agenda and embrace his.

The multifaceted wisdom of God is spread through the entire body, and only as we learn to live in love with one another will we be able to see the fruits of it. No one sees completely. No one has all the answers. Unity is not uniformity; it's harmony. As God transforms us he takes unique expression in each of our personalities and stories. As he brings diverse people together we all get a fuller view of God and what he is like than any of us would see alone. Like a symphony, it is the harmonizing blend of our uniqueness wrapping around his heart and purpose. As we all are tuning to his frequency we will be in tune with one another and the agreement and collaborations it produces can have a profound impact in the world.

This is the dance of growing unity that allows us to reflect one heart, one purpose, and one mind. What Jesus prayed for in John 17, Paul described in more detail in Philippians 4:1–2:

> If you have any encouragement from being united with Christ, if any comfort from his love, if any fellowship with the Spirit, if any tenderness and compassion, then make my joy complete by being like-minded, having the same love, being one in spirit and purpose. Do nothing out of selfish ambition or vain conceit, but in humility consider others better than yourselves. Each of you should look not only to your own interests, but also to the interests of others.

What makes Paul's joy complete? It wasn't in his great exploits for God, but in watching people find their way into the unity that Father gives. They become so enmeshed in the life of God that they have the ability to recognize and turn away from selfish ambition (what we do for profit, power, and privilege) and vain conceit (drawing attention to ourselves in a way that makes us look better than others). They will look beyond what's good for them and also care about what is good for others, and that creates an environment in which the kingdom is put on display. It doesn't take much. Look at his requirements:

If you have any encouragement from being united with Christ... Are you one with him? Do you trust him to change you? Then trust him to shape the others around you.

If any comfort from his love... Do you know Jesus has your back even when others fail you? You will be betrayed. You will be lied to and lied about as people try to manage their pain. Do you know that you're loved enough that God will take care of you?

If any fellowship with the Spirit... Am I doing what I'm doing to get the benefits I anticipate, or am I following him as best I can? Is he big enough to get through to me every day whatever he needs me to do and however he asks me to lay down my life for a greater kingdom?

*If any tenderness and compassion...*Do I have the least bit of affection for the people I'm around so that I am a soft heart for them to engage, and do I care at least as much about their well-being as I care for my own?

Paul doesn't ask for a lot of these things. "If you have *any . . .*" The smallest portion opens up a very wide door to the life of unity. When you recognize these in people, you'll see how easy walking in unity actually is. It will grow out of your love for each other, not necessarily because you see things the same way or are involved in the same activities. Who do you see around you growing in their oneness with Christ? They may be struggling, young on the journey, or even a bit fleshy at times, but are they hungry for him? I know I've found people like that when I see them go against their own self-interest to fulfill a deeper leading in their heart.

This is where conformity-based systems fail. People are so busy conforming to doctrine or rituals that they never find the freedom to ask the difficult questions, find their own journey inside of the new creation, and get to know God in a way that transforms them. They stay underlings in a system designed to keep them safe, but that actually hinders their growth. There's much I disagree with in Bishop John Shelby Sponge's writings, but he's absolutely right when he said, "Religion is in the guilt-producing, control business. The church doesn't like for people to grow up, because you can't control grown-ups." One researcher said that the pedagogy of many Sunday morning services is equal to that of a kindergarten class. Where else as adults do we all file in, sit in rows, sing songs, parrot what we're told, and listen passively to what is being said up front?

Unity comes from those who are learning to follow him and who refuse to exploit people for their own agenda or seek to impose their will on others. That's what Jesus and Paul were talking about, often called "church discipline." It wasn't to banish someone from being loved and shaming them into better choices. It was simply to be honest about the fact that unless we're learning to follow him we cannot share a journey. We can love people lost in self-indulgence, but we can't grow in unity with them.

The fruit of this unity is that we actually become part of God's unfolding purpose in Creation:

> I tell you the truth, whatever you bind on earth will be bound in heaven, and whatever you loose on earth will be loosed in heaven. Again, I tell you that if two of you on earth agree about anything you ask for, it will be done for you by my Father in heaven. For where two or three come together in my name, there am I with them. (Matthew 18:18–20)

Tapping the power of growing unity doesn't demand large groups of people. Jesus said where two or three agree or simply get together in his name amazing things can happen.

Agreement helps us identify truth.

Since we all know in part and see in part, as those parts harmonize together we will get a clearer picture of truth. We all have an amazing capacity for self-deception and to gather information that agrees with what we want to hear and believe. But as we think and explore with others on this journey, Jesus' way of viewing things becomes more evident. While that is valuable in sorting out God's character and purpose, it is also incredibly helpful as we learn to live in that truth in the concrete decisions of life. Am I part of a transformative relationship with him, or simply serving myself hoping God will bless it. Since truth sets us free we'll want to embrace it even if it challenges some of our pet theologies. That's why people growing in Christ want to be in the widest possible conversation and engage people who don't see things exactly the way they do. That includes the writings and thoughts of saints long past, as well as others around them. They don't mind considering someone else's thoughts because they don't see truth as so fragile that they will be easily deceived by contrary views. They are confident truth will win out in the end.

Wherever I disagree with someone growing in Jesus, I realize one of three things is true. Either they're right and I'm wrong and God has more work to do in me. Or, they're wrong and I'm right and he has some work to do in them. Or, and this is most likely, we're both a bit off and he has more work to do in both of us. But as we keep loving and keep listening to each other and to him, we'll come to understand more than we'd ever grasp on our own. Some things will be confirmed; others exposed and overturned as I continue to grow. This is not truth-by-democracy. We each must hold to truth as we see it in our hearts and no one is asked to betray their conscience for an outward show of unity. Instead we trust that as we grow in him we'll also grow together.

Growing agreement allows us to collaborate in anything the Lord gives us to do.

We know God is asking us to do something together when our hearts are in agreement about it. This is the power of decentralized systems. Where there is agreement people can act together even if others might disagree or not support it. In time the fruit of their labor will reveal whether or not God was in it. And if people get it wrong, the impact of it will be far less than if a huge group of people were compelled to go along if their heart wasn't in it.

A few years ago a book on business management called *The Starfish and the Spider: The Unstoppable Power of Leaderless Organizations* provided a powerful image of decentralized structures. The spider represents traditional organizations with CEOs, hierarchical structures, and top-down management. If you cut off the head of a spider it dies. How many large congregations have simply crashed when their charismatic leader died, moved on to something else, or failed? The starfish, however, has no head to cut off. If it loses a leg the starfish grows a new one, and then the leg itself will grow into another starfish because it doesn't have a centralized brain. It is a neural network that can regenerate itself easily.

The authors make the point that decentralized networks are far more resilient and have tremendous power because they are not bogged down by the needs of an infrastructure that will compromise the values of the community. People are more engaged and contributions of those who share a common passion have far more impact than conventional institutional models. These communities prize relationship, engender trust, and pursue a purpose that transcends financial reward. As we'll see in the next chapter, this kind of network frees leadership from the need to manage and puts them in a better position to equip and facilitate others.

What I love about this picture is that the body of Christ functions with the best of both worlds. We do have a head, Jesus himself. But he doesn't lead through an institutional or hierarchical system; he leads everyone personally. This network can function quickly and effectively without the overhead or distraction of a large institution.

Our growing agreement moves heaven and earth. The authority we talked about in the last chapter gets raised significantly where God's people come into agreement. Two or three in agreement with God and each other raise the power of prayer to effectiveness unseen individually.

It was the strangest prayer meeting I'd ever been to. More than a hundred people had gathered and before we started one of the facilitators suggested that we only pray about those things for which we had massive agreement. If someone wanted to pray they were encouraged to tell the group what they wanted to pray. They even took time to discuss some of the suggestions to make sure everyone understood. Then they would ask, "How many of you could agree with this prayer?" They looked for more than 90 percent to nod in agreement. If they didn't get that, they would go on to the next suggestion. It blessed me to see the honesty of people that would affirm some and lovingly shrug off others. There seemed to be no embarrassment when someone was told, "You might be right, but the rest of us don't seem to be there yet."

Checking out requests with others to discern God's will and praying fervently in agreement moves the needle appreciably. Of course our most important agreement is with Jesus and the way he works. This is not the way to get God to give us what we want. I have been in meetings where prayers are offered for the most outrageous things like God stopping some sin from ever happening again in California. Yes, everyone was in agreement, but they weren't praying in tune with God's activity, only their wishes.

Relationships of love allow us to grow in the common-unity Jesus invites us into. By embracing a journey with others, their insights will shape our hearts. Where we don't have agreement, we can tread lightly as we continue to see what more God might want to reveal to us. But in those moments where our hearts merge with his and with others, we taste the awesome joy that God has known in himself for all eternity and tap the unbelievable power that results in transformed lives and circumstances around us.

18

Equipping without Subduing

For we are God's workmanship, created in Christ Jesus to do good works, which God prepared in advance for us to do.

EPHESIANS 2:10

Characteristic Eight:
Everyone is equipped to follow Jesus.

"The harvest is plentiful but the workers are few." (Matthew 9:37) Looking at the crowds of desperate and hungry people with only a handful of followers must have been overwhelming for Jesus. He knew many more workers would be needed.

I remember reading those words thirty years ago and thinking, *My how times have changed.* Then, I saw a myriad of Christian congregations and organizations with an abundance of people seeking to be in full-time ministry, pastor the largest church, or write the next Christian best-seller. There seemed little room at the top in our day, and trying to find my way there I wondered if the tide had turned and we had too many.

But that's when I was thinking like a competitor inside the old creation. Of course people want to be at the top of the heap for the influence and benefits it provides. From Israel's demand for a king to the email I received yesterday from a frustrated pastor whose people won't do what he thinks they should, we are preoccupied with power and how it is disbursed in our world. That is, and has always been, a crowded playing field. But Jesus was looking for workers of a different breed—those who have no interest in building a personal following, but simply want to help others find a full and free life in Jesus and to facilitate the opportunities for honest and genuine friendships to grow. That kind of worker may be as rare in our day as it was in his.

Later, when the disciples argued over who would be the top dogs in Jesus' kingdom, he let them know that they were barking up the wrong tree. In response he taught them about real leadership. The world exploits power to lord over others, and its leaders dole out benefits and punishments to gain more. (Mark 10:42–43) "Not so with you." He didn't so much forbid them to do it, as he was letting them know such use of power had no place in his kingdom. People who come alive in the new creation have neither a desire to manage others or to be managed themselves. They want to learn to listen to him, respond to him, and help others find that same joy.

So the challenge in the new creation is how to equip people without subduing them—teaching them how to follow him rather than making them dependent on our teaching or program. Part of the flavor of the antichrist spirit that John referred to in his letter is not the end-of-the-age personification of evil. He said many antichrists were already in the world. He was referring not to those who were hostile to Christ, but to those who wanted to provide a Christ-substitute, making people dependent on themselves rather than on him.

When I was a pastor I could not understand why those who were most qualified as elders among us would refuse the position when we offered it to them, and why we had so many problems with those who would accept it. I remember asking a man of great maturity and depth to join our elder team. He turned me down, unwilling to spend countless hours in planning meetings instead of helping people grow spiritually. He saw the title and the position we offered, as well as the future staff position we dangled before him, as a detriment to the place he already had in people's lives.

I have the same deference to leadership terms now. I am often asked whether I am an apostle, a teacher, or a pastor. I don't answer the question directly because whatever gift I have among the body of Christ best functions alongside them as a brother. Once people put a label on it, they treat me in ways that diminish my effectiveness. That's what Jesus was driving at in Matthew 23, "But you are not to be called 'Rabbi,' for you have only one Master and you are all brothers." I don't mind functioning as a teacher or elder, but when most people use those terms they are setting me above them in a way that restricts their own growth and diminishes the input I can give them. Instead of letting me help them learn to follow Christ, they want to follow me or my ideas instead.

That's why the term *leadership* is difficult to use inside the new creation. People see it as a management role instead of a gift to help others. So when Paul wrote about elders, overseers, or ministry gifts, he's talking about those who help others mature, not those who manage institutions. And when we take the words of Hebrews to "Obey your leaders and submit to their authority," (13:17) and apply them to old creation constructs, we get distorted views of leadership and end up seeking out the wrong people to lead. How often has this Scripture been used by so-called leaders to great harm as a divine sanction for whatever power they wanted to hold over others? Rather than demanding unquestioned submission, the writer was simply appealing to the younger ones to not make it difficult for their older brothers and sisters to help them grow.

Since leadership language is used so sparingly in the New Testament, translators have to embellish its use to justify the ecclesiastical systems we have constructed over the centuries. As Gayle Erwin, author of *The Jesus Style*, is fond of pointing out, at the feeding of the five thousand the only thing Jesus asked the disciples to do was to be his waiters and his janitors. Later Jesus showed them that true leaders would not rise above to command crowds, but would take the towel and wash the dirty feet of weary travelers.

The greatest among them would be the servant, not the master.

The New Testament teaching and example would resonate more with the word *catalyst* than *leader*. Real elders or overseers are not the people on the platform or manning the denominational office telling others what to do, but they are instead sitting alongside people to equip and encourage them in their own relationship with Jesus. The real task of leaders is not getting people to follow them, but equipping those people to follow Christ. And the real danger is not that people won't listen to them, but that they will become too dependent on their wisdom at the expense of growing in their own relationship to God.

Surprisingly there is little written about how our understanding of leadership shifts inside a new creation, which doesn't need the same management schemes found in the old. That's obviously easier to consider when you only have people to love and not an institution to run. The two will come into conflict more than we'd like to admit, and it's easier to call people to submission than to equip. Almost always the need for a smooth program overrides loving the people it is designed to help.

The reason it is difficult for people to be catalysts of the new creation instead of managers in the old is the very human need for cash, credit, and control. Our old creation systems are shaped by someone's need to earn a living, a seminary's need to draw students, or someone's need to have their preferences rule a corner of the body of Christ. Today, in our celebrity-defined culture, the focus is on creating a platform and branding to draw a following that can create the income stream wanted. However, the drive for money will steadily draw us away from the kingdom. You cannot serve God and money any more today than you could when Jesus warned us not to try. Those who have not yet learned to trust God for their provision won't be helpful in building up the body of Christ. Instead they will carve off their own segment of the faithful thinking their market share will guarantee their success.

Probably for some of these very reasons—cash, credit, and control—the second and third generations of the early church went through a profound shift in their view of leadership. Instead of elders seeing themselves as guardians of the gift of Life among the believers as they cultivated environments of love, grace, and freedom, they became guardians of right theology and practice. Instead of gently instructing people who wanted to know Jesus, they became purveyors of religious systems intended to corral and cajole people into righteousness. No wonder the power and relevance of the church floundered in such institutions.

The new creation invites us back to the previous view, as guardians of the Life of God in people around us. They don't need to build the church, because they trust Jesus to do it. Therefore, they are content to spend their time helping people into a transforming relationship with him. More seasoned in the character of Jesus, these men and women have no need to be up front or to build a following. That's why leadership in his church looks very different from the management skills humans use to build institutions in the old. Promoting the kingdom in the hearts of people usually takes a different skill set: equipping, facilitating, and overseeing.

Equipping. They equip by helping people connect with him and discover how to live in the freedom and life of the new creation. Though seminars and lectures may be able to give some important background, equipping usually happens the same way Jesus did it—spending time with individuals and smaller groups of people so they can engage in the kind of dialog that allows them to discover how God makes himself known to them. You can attend aviation classes and learn all about flying, but you can't learn to fly without an instructor sitting next to you in an airplane.

Facilitating. Since they know that community is a gift God gives, these catalysts simply seed the environment in which community grows by facilitating gatherings, connections, and friendships between people who are learning to live in the new creation. Instead of trying to create community they invite people into their lives and share those friendships generously so that friendships expand around them. This is less about planning regular meetings or building groups, but simply about providing opportunities for relationships to grow. There is no desire to build fences around a certain group that will only factionalize the body of Christ. Instead, by putting people growing to know Jesus into proximity with one another, they prepare the ground for the church to take shape in their locality.

Overseeing. Finally, as overseers in the body of Christ, they don't see themselves as the police—making sure everyone is doing what they are supposed to—but as farmers looking over the field to see what the crops might need to grow. Where is water needed? Where are weeds choking out growth? They are aware of disruptive influence that seeks to destroy the gift of Life, such as someone espousing false teaching, a divisive person pitting people against each other, or someone simply trying to exploit others for their own agenda. They have the courage to approach people personally, honestly, and gently in hopes of showing them a more excellent way. Only if that proves unsuccessful will they warn others to be careful around people who have yet to grasp the reality of the new creation. In a relational network, people are honestly treated for who they are, and if they are disruptive, people will continue to love them, though they will refuse to be exploited by them.

In my experience, real overseers fulfill these tasks not as a job description, but simply because they care deeply about the life of the church having free reign around them. Their actions flow naturally out of the quality of their character, the expression of their gifts, and their passion for his kingdom to spread. They are the fruit of a life well lived, not a role they are trying to fulfill. Having learned how God works in their life, they are able to encourage others in theirs. This is less about managing a program or giving Bible lectures, but becoming a relationally free person able to care about others without any gain for themselves. What does that look like?

First, they walk alongside people having no desire to lord over them. When Jesus sent the Spirit of God to dwell in us, he told us he would be our Comforter or, more literally, "one called alongside to help." If the Spirit himself comes alongside us to help where we allow him to, how do we presume to a higher station than that of anyone else? They don't talk down to people as experts, only as brothers and sisters who may see a bit further down the road.

Second, they are people at rest in themselves, without a vision that others have to fulfill. They reflect both the honesty and gentleness of Christ in helping others see him more clearly. They are not defensive or angry when questioned. They don't push or prod but simply invite people into a better way of living. They are not easily hurt if you don't take their counsel because they realize you're on a journey and trial and error are an important part of it.

Third, they are the person you would want to catch you in your worst moment because they are a soft place to fall. They are full of the comfort that will help you unpack shame and find your way back to Jesus. They will point to truth sweetened with a dependence on Jesus to make the changes that help set you free. They are elders in the truest sense of the word, mature followers of Christ who are engaging and offer wisdom that resonates with his work in you.

Fourth, they are versed in the story of Scripture as well as a listening ear to the Spirit. It's not how much they know that matters, but more importantly how freely they live in it.

Fifth, they are given to hospitality. They are less interested in speaking to masses or starting and perpetuating groups by obligation than they are in inviting people into their lives to learn through friendship, conversation, and example. That's why hospitality is so critical in all of Paul's lists for an overseer and why Jesus saw more value in a lunch with a tax cheat than a healing rally at the stadium. They know that their life, home, and heart are the most impacting venues, not teaching a service or hosting a podcast.

Sixth, they are highly collaborative. They realize the discernment of a few is almost always better than trusting one's insight alone.

Seventh, they feed the hungry, not manipulate the complacent.

They never push truth on people, but invite them into it; thus they gravitate toward those who already want to grow. They are less concerned with entertaining the ninety-nine as finding the one who is lost and helping that one find life. They know growth does not come by compulsion, confident that eventually time and circumstance will turn hearts back to the God we all need.

Elders, pastors, apostles, and teachers provide an amazing service to the body of Christ when they are not the focus of it. When they are unmoored from managing systems, they can give themselves freely to help people learn to live deeply in Christ. Viewing the church as a network of relationships both locally and internationally doesn't negate any of the Scriptures we read about the gifts that help us grow. Those connected in a given area could easily be referred to as the church in Dublin, or Melbourne, or Sacramento. Among those folks some would be recognized as elders, prophets, or apostles by their gifting and the strength of their character—not by a position or title. You can tell someone is living in their gift when people are drawn to the life they live and the wisdom in the heart. Their gift makes room for them but they will never allow others to become dependent on that gift any more than the flight instructor wants his student to always need him.

Catalysts help ignite the process of community, but then it grows from there. They realize that people will be far more engaged when it rises from their own passion and motivation, and the fruit will be far more lasting than following someone else's directive.

19

The New Creation and the Traditional Congregation

From him the whole body, joined and held together by every supporting ligament, grows and builds itself up in love, as each part does its work.

EPHESIANS 4:16

By making room for his church to take shape beyond our traditional congregations, many assume I am hostile toward them. I am not. I have good friends who participate in their local congregations with great enthusiasm, many who serve as pastors and elders. I am often invited to share my heart in congregational settings seeking more relational connections. A lot can happen in that setting that reflects the church Jesus is building, but the institution itself is not the reason for that. When we know that, we'll be far less intrigued with tweaking the machinery than learning to listen to Jesus as our head and to love each other from the heart.

So while a local congregation in and of itself cannot fulfill all that Paul promised us about the church Jesus is building, it can be a place where people discover his reality and engage in the kinds of relationships in which his church takes expression. It's often where people go when they first open to God, and if the teaching is sound, it can provide them with the foundation for a spiritual journey. Corporate expressions of praise and adoration can provide a place for people to engage the transcendent God and opportunities for fellowship can open a door to friendships that can last a lifetime.

However, we'd be less than honest not to wrestle with the fact that their institutional frameworks are remnants of an old creation and thus their priorities are often at odds with the priorities of the new. So while they can facilitate the writing of the creeds to define critical points of theology, an overdependence on them can easily rob people of partaking of God's mystery as he makes himself known in the course of their daily lives. While they do invite people into the freedom of God's grace, they too often negate that grace by loading up an expectation of what it means to be a "good Christian."

As we've seen throughout this book, the new creation thrives in an environment of freedom and love and depends on transformation coming from within, not conformity imposed from without. But that takes time and rare is the man, woman, or institution that can long refuse the urge to give people rules to follow instead of help to discover a transformative relationship with a loving Father. The demands of religion and the needs of an institution for conformity are perfectly aligned so as to make the path of human effort virtually irresistible. It can yield quick results externally, while it saps the vitality of the Gospel.

So while the new creation exists among traditional congregations, the longer a group exists the easier it is to diverge from the purity and simplicity of devotion to Christ into the rigidity of a conformity-based program. Once people become more preoccupied with the success of the congregation than with the unfolding of the kingdom in love, its life will stagnate. Every congregation has to confront the tension between the Spirit's work to seed the life of the new creation and humanity's need to control people for its own reasons.

I have often asked pastors I respect what percentage of their Sunday morning crowd engages the relationship with God they desire for them. I've never heard more than 10 percent. Most attendees seem content to give a weekly nod to God, but are not interested in going too deep in his life. While that's a sad conclusion for the larger group, it does mean that there will be pockets of people in almost every group who are actively engaged with Jesus and his life. If I'm there, those are the people I'm seeking out.

On the darker side are those congregations that are simply fiefdoms for bullies or insecure leaders that take people captive to their will by manipulating them with fear and guilt. I've been in the wake of such groups to help deeply scarred souls find healing. These groups often use the language of radical Christianity and attract passionate people, but that passion is soon twisted into legalism as everyone is told to follow the leader's vision exclusively, to view other groups with disdain, and to abuse others by overtly or covertly marking and shaming people who do not conform. Sadly, some people enjoy abusive congregations, either because it makes them feel superior to "less-committed" believers or because they think their personal spiritual failures merit a weekly berating from the pulpit. Liturgical churches tend to be less manipulative, freer to let you explore your own journey, but they mostly talk of God as if he is remote and not a voice in our daily lives. Those that are newer, more conservative, and evoke more spiritual passion are far more volatile in falling into legalism and pursuing strong personalities instead of following Christ.

What confuses this discussion is the terminology. We have called these institutions "churches" for so long that many have come to believe that they alone are the expression of God's church in the world, whether or not they express the life of the new creation. We can at least say this is true: Just because you attend a congregation or join one, doesn't make you a member of Christ's church any more than joining a golf club makes you a golfer. You may be interested in golf, enjoy watching golf tournaments, and spend time with people who golf. But none of those things makes you a golfer. For that you have to get some clubs, go out on the course, and move that little ball from the tee into the hole on the green. Following Jesus means so much more than sitting in a congregation and assenting to its creed, and I think most conscientious pastors would agree. Just because you are a committed member of a local fellowship does not necessarily mean you are engaging in a transformative relationship with God and growing in deep and honest friendships that can express his reality.

Your quest should not be to find the perfect group or you'll end up all alone. Whether you seek the new creation among a traditional congregation or beyond it, let's return to the analogy we used earlier about the noise-to-signal ratio when tuning an analog radio. As you learn to follow Jesus and live in the reality of the new creation, you'll begin to discern where the signal of his heart is stronger than the noise and static of human engineering. Let's revisit the themes we developed over the previous eight chapters that were designed to help you get a fix on how Jesus works to shape his church.

First, who around you has their attention and affections on Jesus, not on a charismatic leader, author, or an innovative program? Ask people what they like about their congregation and see if "helping them learn to follow Jesus" comes up at the top of the list instead of fawning over the pastor, music team, or children's ministry.

Second, who is learning to live by a growing reliance on God instead of their own effort or achievement? Is the focus on outward conformity or the inner transformation of an affection-based relationship to Jesus? Are you being encouraged to grow in trusting God, or being trained to trust the congregational leadership or program?

Third, who genuinely cares about others and who is not living by obligation, commitment, or covenants? Accountability attempts to change people from the outside and if you are pressured with guilt and fear, you won't grow to know him. Genuine compassion for others spawned by grace working in us will invite us into the most productive relationships.

Fourth, who is open to building friendships and doesn't just invite you to a meeting? Some groups are too large or too busy to provide opportunity for real relationships to grow. Others may already have established friendships that are hard to break in to. Being invited out for a meal is far better than being handed a bulletin with all the meetings you can attend. You want people who are open-hearted and value close, honest friendships that grow in affection and mutual care. You'll see that as they take an interest in you.

Fifth, in whatever group you find, is everyone respected or is there a hierarchy of spirituality that elevates some over others? Do people talk down to you as experts or laterally with you as fellow travelers on a journey of faith?

Sixth, does it find freedom and order in mutual respect and love or by the demands of leadership? How are you treated if you see things differently than others? One of the earmarks of broken leadership is their demand for conformity and their appeals to personal loyalty if you express concerns or ask questions. If they get angry, belittle you ("If that were true don't you think God would tell me first?"), gossip about you, or marginalize you unless you silently submit, you're in a dangerous environment. Run! To grow you need to question what you need to question and struggle where you need to struggle in an environment of love. Of course that also means you will find respectful and appropriate ways to express your concerns so as not to be divisive or undermine other people's freedom as well.

Seventh, are you encouraged to respond wholeheartedly as God leads you and to have relationships with other believers beyond that group? Find the environment where you're free to make mistakes as you learn to listen to his Spirit, and spend time with those who encourage you to follow your heart more than meet their expectations.

Eighth, are people being equipped to have their own spiritual journey, or are they encouraged to be dependent on the leaders? If they forbid you to read books that make them uncomfortable or if you are told you will whither spiritually if you don't regularly fill your tank at the meetings, you're already being taught to be more secure under human leadership than from following Jesus.

Perhaps the best way to tell if you're in a healthy environment is to take your internal temperature every few months. Is your heart growing increasingly full and is God becoming clearer to you, or are you finding yourself exhausted and no closer to God than you were months before? As best you can, ignore the institutional chatter especially if it is laden with guilt and commitment. I find the most fulfilling relationships in a congregation tend to avoid the politics of leadership teams and planning groups because that's where manipulation and obligation first assert themselves to keep control of the group. In the end each of us has to decide at what point the institutional side of congregational life overruns the relational side. When it gets to the point that you spend more time recovering from a service than it took to get ready for it, maybe it's time to disengage from that system. Only you can decide how much relationship you can enjoy with Jesus and others without being lured into the shame-based manipulation religion is notorious for.

I don't look down on those who participate in traditional congregations as if they have accepted a less genuine kingdom or are less passionate about God's love. If their involvement with a congregation invites them deeper into God's reality and connects them to others in real and honest ways, then I am honored to be standing alongside them as fellow-heirs of God's life. For instance, though I think the Catholic system has a host of problems, two priests have greatly inspired my own journey. I am deeply touched by the perspectives of Richard Rohr and blown away by the example of Peter Boyle loving gang kids in the heart of Los Angeles. His *Tattoos on the Heart* is the most inspiring story of love and sharing in the most difficult of circumstances since the Gospel itself.

It's always a joy for me to find people so immersed in the reality of Father's affection in systems that can easily overwhelm it. I'm grateful God makes himself known everywhere and it reminds me that he is so much bigger than the religious systems in which we have sought to encase him. If you look carefully you can find people who express the reality of his church almost anywhere, inside and outside of established congregations. So if you can't find a group that's healthy, look for individuals among them who are on a better journey—especially if they seem a bit out of place in all the machinery. Take your time. There are genuine people with a hunger for God in such places, but they are not always easy to find and relationships in a high-energy environment take a long time to build.

What's important is that each of us are engaged with him and expressing him however he asks us to do so. Let's celebrate the life of the church wherever we find it in people who live generously and graciously. Some stay faithful in local congregations that are replete with religious performance, but do so for reasons of family, habit, or culture, even though they hunger for a reality far beyond it. They faithfully follow God and love his people even though they see through the foibles of the religious system around them. Often they are on the fringes, regarded with suspicion by those who are threatened by their free spirit, but they are jewels in the Father's family.

Of course if you have the influence to help shape the life of a group and invite it back to dynamics more in keeping with the new creation, by all means give it a try. Don't force it on those who don't want it, however. The kingdom does not come by compulsion. I know pastors and elders who would love to dismantle much of the machinery and embrace the realities described in this book. It isn't easy and can only come through heartfelt dialogue. It rarely works, but those who can facilitate that conversation without being judgmental offer the opportunity for a renewal of life and passion.

If you don't have that voice, you can still express your desires to those who do. Again, don't force your way or wait until you're so angry you only make them defensive. Realize that the hope of reformation often falls on deaf years. People like it that way or they wouldn't be there.

If you find you no longer fit in, feel free to move on. A commitment to a congregation is not a life sentence. When it ceases to inspire your life in Jesus, it is time to move on and see what else God has for you. That may come in seasons of great pain, as you come to realize what God is stirring in you no longer fits the group you've been in; it may come with great joy, as God draws you into other opportunities more consistent with his work in you. It would be best not to leave with a volley of condemnation, nor to try to drag others with you. Just follow him as he leads you.

Those who are worried only about the success of their group rather than building up the whole body of Christ will find this discussion threatening. They have even coined the accusation "church hopping" to discourage people from considering leaving their group. I was amused a few years ago when Willow Creek Community Church outside Chicago discovered that many of their more mature participants were no longer as faithful in their Sunday morning attendance as they had been. Instead of celebrating their "graduation" as any university would have done, they saw it as a problem and set about to devise a program that would rein them back in to more consistent attendance.

Maybe we were never meant to be in the same group for life. Those who care most for church as a whole will realize there is great value in a fluidity of church life that allows you to walk alongside different people in different seasons of life. The idea that any one congregation can fully express the life of Jesus in a community is laughable. It takes us all, loving one another beyond the boundaries of any one group and finding a way to share his life and wisdom together. The cross-pollination of people connecting from different backgrounds and linked to different networks of people can fulfill the promise that the church will reflect the multifaceted nature of God and a unity that man cannot create.

If we were all more concerned about that and less concerned about what institution someone does or doesn't attend, we would be freer to participate in his church as it takes shape around us. We all struggle with challenges to live out this journey and we are constantly distracted by religion, the world, and even our sincere efforts for God. Staying true to the kingdom is a challenge for us all.

If you can't find his church among the congregations you know, then maybe it is time to look beyond it and discover that there are so many ways to be part of his church.

20 | Beyond the Congregation

> Now you are the body of Christ, and each one of you is a part of it.
>
> I CORINTHIANS 12:27

F inding a traditional congregation isn't any more difficult than finding a McDonald's hamburger. They are everywhere and they are not subtle about it, with ever-taller steeples and bell towers that intrude into the cityscape. But what do you do if you no longer fit into those conformity-based structures? How do you find the church Jesus is building if there's no sign on the door?

I never foresaw the day when I'd no longer be an active member of a local congregation and getting here hasn't been easy. As much as I respect those who still find it an important part of their spiritual life, it is no longer an important part of mine. Both of the congregations I was part of in my adult years hit a glass ceiling where the institutional needs came in conflict with the life of Jesus I was seeking. I wasn't ready to give up on the desire to participate in his church as a vibrant community of friends cooperating with God's unfolding work in the world, and I discovered that I could have a more fruitful connection with people and share Jesus' life more freely without all the accoutrements, political intrigue, and routine that our institutions force on fellowship.

Most people who leave end up doing what I did, looking for

another group to fill the Sunday morning void and the friendships they lost by leaving. During the last couple of decades, many have found their way into home groups and other more informal gatherings. When they come together to give rise to a community of friends sharing the life of Jesus and his heart for those around them, they can be wonderful places for the church to find expression. A home or sharing a meal is the most natural environment for us to experience his family as we focus on him and his work in us, rather than the meeting.

Unfortunately, however, an entire industry has emerged in trying to make them just another system. Sometimes called house church, simple church, or organic church, books and articles tout them as the model most consistent with the first-century church. These groups meet weekly in a home often beginning with a meal and then sharing a similar ritual to many congregations with a mix of songs, Bible study, prayer, and planning activities. While such gatherings offer the potential for a deeper relational connection, however, it doesn't always pan out that way.

I've been in home groups that had more hoops to jump through than many congregations. One even had rows of folding chairs with an aisle down the middle and a lectern and piano in front of a lighted cross on the wall. House church, indeed! While most aren't like that, it did serve as a metaphor for the many house churches that use the same dynamics of conformity to control people. Control in a small group is even more destructive. Just because people gather in smaller groups and meet in homes doesn't make them immune from the concerns expressed in the last chapter about more traditional congregations. House churches, too, can practice religious performance and miss out on life in Christ, be captive to insecurity, and copy a model instead of following the Master to end up just as much an expression of human effort.

In hopes of creating an international movement a lot of time and money has been invested in refining the program, identifying spokespeople, and hosting conventions in hopes of spreading a house church model as an end-time hope to revitalize the church. As much as I have enjoyed and love the people I've met in that conversation, I'm afraid they are falling into the same traps that originally drove them to house church. I've watched these people compete for visibility and influence, push their pet programs and books, and try to build a leadership-dependent infrastructure.

The problem is not the venue; it is our preoccupation with anything other than him. Any time we try to replicate a human system, it will eventually lead people away from the new creation. Even things that start out with a lot of grace and freedom quickly become pressure-filled with obligations and expectations. Real relationships don't need them, and utilizing them rarely fixes the problem. As with any other expression of the church, enjoy it as long as it expresses his kingdom and give it a wide berth when it no longer does.

"We've stopped going to church and are going to start something in our home this week. Can you give us any tips as to what we might do and what we might want to avoid?" I get that email almost every week. My counsel is always the same: Avoid starting something. Once you start some "thing" your focus will shift from connecting with people to ensuring that the "thing" goes well. Home groups, with a nucleus of people who are looking for something different, are easy to start but they are difficult to sustain when the focus is on a meeting. People will eventually grow bored with house meetings but they won't grow bored with one another if friendship is engaged.

You will find the church easiest when you stop looking for an "it," and simply love the people God has put around you. Start with growing friendships instead of trying to find a group to join. It was no accident that the church began at Pentecost without any strategy or preconceived notion of what it would look like. They weren't told to start Sunday services or have midweek home groups. They simply did what their new experience with the Gospel and their engagement with his Spirit led them to do. Learn to follow him and then engage others around you with the reality of his kingdom and watch how that bears fruit.

At least as Luke recorded it, the early church didn't ever go out to plant churches. Their passion was to make the Gospel clear and to help people grow to know the life Jesus gives. Quite naturally, those learning to follow him ended up in friendships together. It wasn't until years later that the early apostles returned to recognize the church had taken expression among them. You can't plant Jesus' church. He's already done that.

So what do you do if you want to find relational expressions of the church in your life? Interestingly enough, what I share here is as applicable to people who are outside congregational life as those who are in it:

First, remember where church begins—inside of you! We've gotten used to the idea that the church is a location, often with a ready-made program so you can show up and join. If the church is the community of the loved, then it has to begin inside our own hearts where we learn what it means to engage Jesus out of love and pass that love along to others. That's why he asked us to help disciple people, not herd them into groups. You may already know of a more relational group in your area or you might stumble across one, but don't look too hard. God knows how best to care for you. We find his church by first finding him.

Many are surprised to discover that once they leave their previous congregation, they are cut off from those friendships. Depending on how religious the group was or how insecure the leadership, they may have been trained to treat you as suspicious or independent, or even to punish you for leaving by withdrawing their friendship in hopes that you will repent and return. Other groups, while not so vindictive, are usually too busy to make room for someone not at their meetings. Once you're out of sight, you are also out of mind.

That's why many people battle loneliness in the early stages of this journey, especially if they have to start over building friendships that champion the new creation. That takes time. Fortunately, the answer for loneliness is not being around more people but letting God fill that space in your heart. When we try to fill it with people, our relationships will be based on our needs and they'll get twisted before they begin. God often finds it helpful to draw people to himself for a season as they detox from religious performance and seeking the approval of others. As he builds a life with you, you'll be free to love others in a way that will allow healthy friendships to grow.

It often helps to seek out an older brother or sister who is capable of encouraging you into that relationship without adding the religious twist. God can do this in our hearts, but it is so much more fun to be in a conversation with someone else. As you grow in your connection with him, keep in mind that there will be others behind you that you can bless with your help and friendship. Jesus intended his life to be passed along person-to-person, not through classes and curricula.

Second, embrace the desire to engage in the community he's building. As you learn to embrace his affection, you'll soon find your heart turning toward others. Don't worry you'll become a lone ranger. God is a community, and from knowing him you will hunger for his community as well. You'll find yourself connecting with others quite naturally, not based on a mutual need for something called "church," but as the fruit of your passion for him and his unfolding kingdom. That's when you'll discover that his church is already surrounding you.

You don't have to look any further than the people you already know—family, friends, co-workers, neighbors, and even strangers you might engage with briefly on a bus or at the market. Each day, love whomever God puts before you and see where it leads. Help those who have a need, befriend someone who's lonely, and be gracious to all. Sometimes a simple greeting starts a conversation.

The more authentically you learn to live, the less need you'll have to control these conversations. You'll find yourself genuinely caring for the people around you and freer to do what love draws you to do. Out of the vast array of those conversations, you'll find yourself more drawn to some than others. You'll want to find time to engage them, either over coffee or for a meal. Follow your heart here and make room in your life for them. You don't have to create special times for this. You can do the things together that are already part of your life—eating, running errands, household projects, sports or other recreational activities. Some of these relationships will continue to grow; others may just be for a brief season.

Third, avoid what feels religiously artificial. When Sara and I found ourselves outside the congregational lifestyle, we felt the pressure to organize something to replace what we had lost. We even had some discussion about starting another congregation that would embrace more relational priorities. But everything we tried felt a bit awkward and artificial. We could feel the environment change just in moving from a meal with a free-flowing conversation of friends, to the formality of starting a meeting together. We were sharing great conversations about our spiritual journeys, but as soon as we tried to fit that into a meeting the dialogue grew stilted.

We finally gave up the meetings and continued our friendships as we stumbled into a growing conversation about his transforming life in us. That pool of relationship provided all the opportunity we needed to continue to grow in Jesus, to explore what church might look like, and to care for others as each had need or resource. I watched that circle of friends grow, not only with new local people who shared our passion, but also with people around the world.

Five years later we had the chance to do it all over again. We moved 200 miles south into an area of Southern California where we knew no one. Since we wanted to continue this journey outside the traditional congregation, we had a new challenge. How do we meet other followers of Jesus if we don't attend a local fellowship? We continued to follow him and simply love the people God put around us. We got to know our neighbors and though none of them were passionate followers of Jesus at the time, all had some spiritual curiosity that came up in our growing friendship. We always kept our ears open for people who wanted to connect more deeply with Jesus and to God's nudges to involve ourselves in the city as opportunities emerged. I volunteered to help out the local mission, and at one point we were drawn to connect with a small fellowship that was coming unraveled after their pastor's moral failure. We found them endearing and stayed for a season as they asked us to help them explore an authentic life in Jesus.

Our connection with his church became richer than it would have if we attended the same meeting every week. The Spirit sets you in the family by putting the people around you he wants you to know, or he can nudge you to engage others the way we did. You might hear about a small group fellowship, prayer breakfast, or outreach that tugs at your heart. It's not about the meeting, but the people.

It can happen in so many ways. I met a man who lived in a remote location and knew no one with whom he could share his life in Jesus. One day he lost his wallet in a mall a hundred miles away. He didn't realize it until he got home. He called the mall and no one had turned it in. Two hours later he got a call from a local family. They found his wallet and, noticing he lived in the same town they did, decided to bring it back to him. As they exchanged the wallet they found they'd both been praying for the same kind of connection and began a journey together.

I'm not suggesting you toss your wallet into a mall and see what happens, but it shows that God has an infinite number of ways to connect his people. I know a young mom who found her way into a group of moms and kids that got together regularly because she overheard two women talking about it in line at the grocery store. She was new in the city and hoping to meet some other moms. As she inquired more, they invited her to come and bring her children. It was not a Christian group, but this young mother has found great friendship there and now some of those moms have found their way into a relationship with God and have become a source of great fellowship to her.

I've traveled halfway around the world to share some of my journey with people who invited me, only for them to discover that there were others in town they did not know and who became fast friends after I left. As you navigate through life, keep your eyes and ears open. If something draws you, give it a try and see what you find there. Small group studies, recreation groups, breakfast groups, or para-church outreaches are excellent places to meet people and get to know them as you share a task together. I've even hosted Bible studies for a limited time in my home with a few friends and watched as others heard about it and wanted to join us.

Fourth, be intentional about relationships. All we have to do is be aware of his moving in the people around us and gravitate to those moments that are real and engaging. Which conversations empower you to live more deeply in his love, inspire you to greater trust, and set you at ease in his working?

The possibilities are literally limitless.

Who stimulates your journey in Christ? Spend time with them.

Who needs a friend (believer or not)? Befriend them.

Who needs help connecting with God? Help them.

A few years ago I sat with a group of thirty people who were part of a "church plant." They had purchased a coffee shop so the profits could serve the poor, and then they met there weekly for service. One month each summer they take a break from their Sunday meeting and I was with them as that month was concluding. They were perplexed. They told stories of how powerful their last month had been and the amount of growth they'd all experienced. They wanted me to help them explore ways to make their weekly meeting more engaging and relevant.

"If I were you," I responded, "I wouldn't even try. I suspect the life of the church lies down the pathway you've been on the last month, not trying to figure a way to shoehorn that into a weekly meeting." I reminded them that Jesus didn't spend his life in a lot of preplanned meetings and he touched people most deeply in life as it unfolded around him.

Church is not the means to an end; it is the fruit of those thriving in him. Go down that road. Yes, it is easier to plan a meeting than make friends. The latter requires significant intentionality on our part—to go where others are, to strike up a conversation, and to recognize those relationships God is inviting you into more deeply. As we grow secure in his love we'll find ourselves increasingly free to engage others not for what we can get out of it, but simply to be a blessing to them. The best friendships begin here. You don't have to force your way in. If God is making the connection, they will desire it as well.

From all of those places and many others, we enjoy a growing circle of friends that share a wide conversation about life in Jesus. None of us feel the need to organize any kind of weekly meeting; we just continue to grow in Christ and in friendship with one another. There are times he asks us to do tasks together and we've watched the church take expression among us, both in ways that have touched an area and in ways that have touched others around the world.

Fifth, be generous with your friendships. With every overlapping relationship, the church grows. One of the greatest treasures I can share with someone I love is access to my other friends. This is the final step in the temple rising. The Spirit weaves a tapestry of light and life in the world by knitting together an international network of interrelated people whose relationships give visibility to the work of Jesus. As people generously share their friendships instead of becoming cloistered in their own groups, the church takes shape.

I am blessed to have good friends across a wide spectrum of the body of Christ, locally, nationally, and internationally. I spend time with people who go to and even lead traditional congregations, those committed to the house church movement, and those who simply live out their life relationally in the body of Christ. Not only am I blessed by wisdom from such a diverse group, but the revelation of the body of Christ is enhanced by a growing unity of heart that is greater than whether or not we share conformity to a given group.

His church is an ever-expanding network of friends and friends of friends that Jesus arranges so he can bring wisdom, resources, and his kingdom to bear on the world. I've been blessed to have a front row seat for some of the most amazing connections that allowed some higher purpose of his to unfold because we had the time and flexibility to work together at his request.

Participating in his church for us now is simply asking him each week, "Who do you want us to be with?" As people are on our heart, we make time to be with them for whatever purpose he has in mind. We can be helping people find their way out of a dark place, equipping people to embrace their own relationship with him, enjoying the fellowship of people exploring a vast kingdom as they share their experiences and hopes, learning together something we need to know, helping others connect with people we know, or finding agreement that allows the will of God to come to this earth as it already functions in heaven.

That's how the church finds expression. Don't look to be loved, love! Don't look for like-minded people, just those he's asking you to walk alongside. Live that way and you'll find the church taking shape around you.

It can really be that simple…and that real!

21 | The Difficult Questions

The only thing that counts is faith expressing itself through love.

GALATIANS 5:6

hroughout this book I've shared lots of examples of how his community can take shape, from a conversation of two or three over a meal, to people who gather around a hospitable household, to projects God invites us into to help the world around us, to international gatherings to build new friendships, to providing a study or other opportunity for people to connect and grow in their own spiritual journey, to the relationships spawned in more traditional congregations. They can gather weekly or more spontaneously.

His church is not made up of the activities we're doing; what matters most is how we treat one another. The church appears where people engage in relationships of affection, genuineness, wisdom, and generosity. While we cannot build his church for him, we find our place in it by learning to live in his love and sharing it freely with others. Don't let your expectations focus on any one particular outcome, or you may miss her when she's right in front of you. His church can take on a thousand different expressions, which is why it is useless to copy someone else's model.

Twenty years ago as a congregational pastor, I could not have conceived of the incredible tapestry of his church growing beyond my own version of it. I couldn't imagine a church without "worship" services, Sunday school, offerings, or full-time staff. How would people be taught or led? How would community happen? How would children learn about God? How would we know who elders are? Notice how many questions emerge the minute we question the essentiality of our congregational systems.

The questions themselves show how dependent we've become on those institutions for our spiritual survival. We cannot imagine that Jesus is able to move beyond them in touching our lives, our children, or the world. Losing our dependency on human systems is scary at the start because we've been taught to trust them. I even worried that I might be wrong and by sharing my journey I might lead others astray. I know there are many who wish I'd heeded that last impulse and not stirred up such a hornet's nest. But honestly, you have no idea what you will come to discover about Jesus and his church after being out of a conformity-based system for a few years.

Having learned to live more relationally for nearly two decades, my perspective has completely shifted. Now it is harder for me to see how our institutions can give rise to the relational realities in which his church thrives. Now I wonder how weekly Bible lectures alone can possibly help people engage God. How are children ever going to learn about him in a Sunday school curriculum that turns every Bible story into a morality play that indoctrinates them into believing their behavior is more important to God than they are? And I don't know how people can possibly enjoy the gift of an elder coming alongside them when they are so busy managing an institution.

All that Scripture teaches us about his church is far better lived relationally. I've been asked hundreds of questions by those losing their trust in religious systems, but I haven't a clue how else to engage his church. I could take a chapter each to explore the ramifications of the questions I am most asked, but that would turn this into a how-to book and wouldn't do us any good. So rather than answer exhaustively, I'm going to make a few comments about each question that I hope will help you peek into a wider world where you can explore these questions in your own relationship with him and with others.

Don't I need to be taught? In a word, no! The purpose of the New Covenant was to invite each of us into a growing relationship with Jesus so that we have no need to be taught by others. He wants to lead you into God's truth. Don't ever give that away to another human being, which means each of us will have to discern between truth and error. We need to learn to recognize the fragrance of Father and turn away from that which may tickle our ears but only draw our dependency away from him. But just because teaching isn't necessary doesn't mean it isn't a valuable supplement to the Spirit's leading. There are so many ways for you to find teaching that will help you understand more about God, the Scriptures, and his purpose—taking classes, joining a Bible study, reading books, hosting a retreat, or pursuing courses online. As a teacher myself, I enjoy the variety of venues in which teaching can occur, but if someone isn't already listening to him then any teaching will only be a transfer of information and not bear the fruit of life.

How will our children learn about God? They will learn as they always have, from the example of their parents. Sunday school has always been overrated as a discipleship tool. Introducing your children to Jesus is like introducing them to their grandma. You didn't teach them a biography first; you just introduce them to each other. Don't teach your children to be good Christians, show them how to walk with God in the same way you do. From the youngest ages, they can see God as a part of the family as they pray, share, and learn together what it means to follow him. As they get older their interactions with other adults and older children can also reinforce their own journey where they are free to question and discover their own relationship with him.

Don't we need to worship with others? The Sunday morning service with its liturgy can be exhilarating spiritually, but it is not a requirement or a means of grace. Worship isn't singing or public prayers anyway; it's a life lived under Father's care. It goes on every day, not just Sunday. If you enjoy singing and adoration, avail yourself of the opportunity. But it doesn't make you more spiritual than someone who doesn't. Everything valuable about our Sunday experiences can be lived out in more relational settings where they may have less entertainment value but will be far more engaging spiritually.

What about communion? For the first three hundred years of its existence, the church would not have conceived of sharing the Lord's Supper at any place other than the family dining room. That's the only place they met and as they shared a meal they celebrated his presence among them with bread and wine. You can share it together in informal settings wherever Christ's body gathers.

What about tithing and giving? The follower of Jesus is not under any obligation to tithe. That was an Old Testament construct for the Jewish people to provide for their national life. While tithing predated the Old Covenant, it was not an obligation for Abraham but a gift of thanksgiving. That said, the activities of the Old Covenant were, in the words of the letter to the Hebrews, a shadow of a greater reality. In 2 Corinthians 8–9, Paul gets behind the shadow to God's heart about giving. As an obligation it is fruitless. Giving is the fruit of living in God's generosity. When you know God has been generous with you, you will be generous with others and 10 percent will seem like a very cheap substitute.

If, however, you attend and benefit from a traditional congregation, realize that it takes a significant number of people giving 10 percent of their income to meet expenses. If you enjoy the benefits, it would only be fair to help with the costs. I don't see that as tithing or even giving to God, only sharing expenses for what you enjoy together.

When you live generously you will find ample opportunity to help the needy and to support his kingdom as it reveals itself among us. That can mean filling up a gas tank for a single mom, contributing to an orphanage overseas, inviting the neighborhood over for dinner, supporting someone whose gift helps others come alive in Christ, or a zillion other ways Jesus would want to express his generosity through you. I know one man who puts a significant amount of money in his wallet each month and looks for people to share it with all month long. He doesn't get a tax deduction for it, but he lives generously in the world.

Where can I use my teaching/music gift? Many enjoy being on the stage teaching or leading songs before an appreciative crowd. Giving up that stage is not easy for some, but that is not the only place such gifts and passion can be exercised. Many have found it far more incarnational to take their gifts into the street, parks, retirement homes, and coffeehouses. God can find some incredible ways to share your gifts other than making it the focus of the community.

Don't we have to have elders? It's not a matter of having to. There *are* elders in Christ's family, those who are a bit further down the road and available to help others learn to walk with God. They don't have to be appointed by a group to make it official; their wisdom and character point them out. They are not elders of institutions, but servants among his people. It may be helpful at times to point out true elders in a community as Paul asked Timothy to do, so that newer followers can learn to discern the true from the false.

What about full-time ministry? That's a strange designation isn't it, since we are all full-time followers of Jesus? What we do for a living is just God's way of putting us near people he wants us to be with and to provide for our daily necessities. In relational community there isn't enough work for people to be on a paid staff. But it is true that some whose gifts in equipping others and encouraging his church have more opportunity than their vocation allows them to be available and Jesus can care for them through the generosity of the community or in lots of other ways. Let them trust Jesus for their resource, and not burden others with guilt or obligation.

How will people be cared for? If every one of us cares for the people God puts near us there would be plenty of ministry to go around for the poor, the elderly, and the broken. It's not a matter of inviting them to a meeting, but going where they are. Who is in your path today that needs encouragement, love, or help with the brutalities of life? Get involved; don't just find them a ministry to do it for you. When our available resource is greater than our reach, our generosity can bless others whose reach to others exceeds their available resource.

What about church discipline? I'm certain that the discipline process of Matthew 18 was never to be applied in an institutional setting. I've never seen it done that didn't result in abusive treatment, designed to manipulate people's responses out of fear instead of inviting them into transformation and freedom. The things I had to do as a pastor to protect the environment now make me cringe with regret. The language of Matthew 18 and I Corinthians 5 are far more powerful inside a community of friends. If someone we're walking with is no longer honoring the environment of following Jesus, a private conversation to reach out in love is in order. If they refuse to listen then a few others can get involved. If they continue their destructive ways the others can be told about it to restrict their influence, not to shame them with rejection.

Jesus told us to let the wheat and tares grow up together and we have no business trying to sort them out. Not having something to manage, I no longer have to spend my time trying to decide who is in and who is out. The church is built on the confidence that God knows those who are his (2 Timothy 2:19), so we don't have to make that determination. We are free to love everyone and see what God might do as a result.

How do we know who is a Christian if they don't belong to a recognized group? My question now is how do we know if they do? Many people are part of congregations for social, religious, or cultural reasons, but have no desire to follow Jesus. We know someone belongs to him not by the group they identify with, but by the love and life of Jesus that emanates from them. It is not so hard to tell in most cases.

What about mission and evangelism? The vast majority of people who come to Christ even at an organized outreach do so because of the influence of a friend who was with them in a propitious moment of need or crisis. Rather than thinking the lost have to find a church to go to, we are alongside them in the world demonstrating Christ to them. It is far more powerful. During the last twenty years, I've been part of helping lots of people go out in various missions as well as helping indigenous people have the tools they need to be a blessing in their own community. Without any overhead costs people cooperating with Jesus will be led and supported for a variety of endeavors.

What about weddings, baptisms, and funerals? The last two don't require any ordination. Anyone who knows Jesus can baptize, and anyone can preside at a funeral. Weddings are a bit trickier, depending on the laws where you live. If a young couple doesn't know anyone authorized to officiate at the wedding, I encourage them to satisfy the requirements of the state in a civil ceremony at the courthouse and then hold a real wedding celebration with their friends and family where the person the couple most desires can preside over the festivities.

How will we work together without coordinating institutions? Jesus has an amazing ability to knit his people together at just the right time to share gifts and resources that can accomplish extraordinary things. Throughout the past twenty years I've had a front row seat to watch coordination and collaborations emerge that no human could have foreseen and brought into existence. Just in the last six months, I've watched God bring together the resources of my friends in the West with some needs of my friends in east Africa, putting more than a quarter of a million dollars to rescue 120,000 people dying of starvation and disease in a severe drought. We were able to empower volunteers to take food and medicine to them as well as hire a company to drill three wells where none existed.

It all started with a disillusioned young preacher, desperate for something more than he had known searching the Internet to download a free copy of *He Loves Me* that revitalized his heart. He invited me to Kenya, which began a three-year exchange to see if that might be in Father's heart. While we were sorting that out, I got a recommendation from a missionary in Kenya I bumped into who told me this man had a heart of gold and I could trust him. Eventually I went to Kenya, met many of the people, and was captured by their hearts and the desperate conditions they lived under. We began an orphanage there for kids growing up in their own filth and learned to work together over something small. Then, at the beginning of this year, some of our friends in Kenya heard stories of a large group of people north of them who were dying, with no government services or NGO presence. We sent them with $62,000 for water, food, and medicine that Kenyan volunteers wanted to take to them. That didn't turn out to be enough and they wanted to go back as volunteers to build schools, wells, and a dispensary to help turn their economy around and preserve their lives. Could we supply the materials so they could do the building? Unbeknownst to me, a couple from Texas at God's leading had been putting money into an account for years without knowing why. When they heard about the need in Kenya, they called me to underwrite $155,000 of the work there.

Look at all the threads God pulled together over years, to create a worldwide network that could bring need, resource, and manpower together in a moment's notice. When people tell me we need large institutions to have any impact, I know of too many stories like this one that demonstrate how simple it is for God to knit his people together through simple obedience. Without administrative fees or fundraising plans, he brought resources together to rescue 120,000 people dying on the plains of Kenya, and he opened their hearts to the Gospel.

What if everyone leaves his or her institution, what becomes of Christianity, then? That's a good question, but a hypothetical one that is incredibly unlikely. While the demographics are not promising for the future, institutions always find a way to survive. I suspect most people who are content there won't even risk reading a book like this.

Yes, there is a vast pasture of God's life and provision to be explored beyond the conformity of our institutions. It is a risk, to be sure, but one with incredible rewards. Perhaps the biggest change is that it forces people to move from being a passive part in someone else's machine, to someone who actively participates in his unfolding kingdom. You don't get to follow someone else's instructions anymore, but instead you have to be more intentional in all aspects of connecting with him and his church.

But those are the sheep I want to romp with in the Father's care. What can happen out of that simple reality could set a world on fire, just like it did the first time.

22

To Be Continued

I do not consider myself yet to have taken
hold of it. But one thing I do: Forgetting
what is behind and straining toward what is
ahead, I press on...

PHILIPPIANS 3:13

No, this is not a promise for a sequel called *Finding Church Too!* I am simply acknowledging that this book speaks into a story that is far from complete. Though Jesus is building his church, she is not yet all that she will be to bring this age to its conclusion and to be presented to him as his spotless bride. And while I'm filled with anticipation at what might yet lie down the road, I have no idea what this glorious worldwide family will look like in the end as more people are untangled from religious obligation and learn to live in the reality of his love.

The local and international tastes I've had of this church when people are following him and living generously with one another have fulfilled my understanding of Scripture and the desires it spawned. If I died tomorrow I could truthfully say that I've seen the incredible beauty and power of his church that I always hoped was possible. Now my heart yearns to see more of his children find their way into that reality, and when they do I can't imagine all the ways she will be revealed.

I told you up front that I wasn't an expert with all of the answers and now that we've arrived at the final chapter, hopefully you're convinced. I've just paused at this point of my journey to record what I have discovered to date. If you have more questions than answers, you are not alone. I do too, so I will continue to discover how I can more effectively engage this church Jesus is building. I relish the continuing lifelong adventure of seeing his church expand around me and in the earth.

I pray it continues to unfold in your journey as well. I hope many of you arrive at the end of this book as exhilarated as I am by the possibilities of finding a more vibrant church experience than you have found to date. If you've wondered why you never seemed to fit into the human models we've created, perhaps now you understand why. You weren't rebellious or independent; you just had a seed of life in your heart that refused to settle for an illusion when something real beckoned you onward.

I realize some of you might be frustrated that I've not given you the clear actions you should implement so that you can enjoy his church as well. With each turn of the page, you were hoping I'd finally get to the how-to list that you could follow. Honestly, if I had such a list, I'd share it with you. I find no joy in frustrating people with unfulfilled hunger. However, I know that any list I would give would be fraudulent. We can't chart her in intellectual terms and then implement our own strategies to make her appear. We would only end up focused on our work instead of his and then blame ourselves for not doing it well enough.

Finding church is not a matter of locating a group of Christians you enjoy and joining in. I've said all along that his church is the fruit borne among the lives of those who are learning to live in his love and follow his voice. To find her you have to embrace him and discover how to live and think alongside others in the new creation. This is not a process we control; we can only follow him each day as we trust him to connect the dots.

That's why I hope this book inspires a broader conversation of men and women who are passionate about his kingdom and are willing to look beyond our differences to the common unity we have simply because we are children of the same Father. I hope people in subsequent generations will engage the dialogue and build on it, taking it further than my generation has. I've had to unlearn so much to find my way back to a reality I wish I had engaged at a much younger age. The people I see now in their twenties and thirties who are learning to live in his love and in growing trust in his work give me great hope that the best discoveries are still ahead.

This conversation won't be about the best way to do church, or to which one you belong, but how can we belong more fully to Jesus and demonstrate the reality of his kingdom. How can he be our shepherd individually and collectively so that we can truly share the unity that Father, Son, and Spirit have enjoyed for all eternity? How can we encourage one another on that path, and how might he connect us in conversations and collaborations of generosity and graciousness that will make him visible?

To have it, however, we will have to lay down our own kingdoms and the agendas we hold for others. There will be many who won't be able to do that, and they will feel threatened enough that they will distance themselves from the conversation instead of joining it. They will twist and mock my words to defend their own limited view of the church and will seek to marginalize those who dare to dream beyond the borders they have set. Give them a wide berth and don't let them detract you from following the passion in your heart. Christianity has spawned an entire industry of congregations, seminaries, publications, and denominations, all of which have turf to protect to guarantee their survival. They want people to stay dependent on them and thus promote a fear-based Christianity that considers belonging to the wrong "church" or believing the wrong doctrine as a cause for divine rejection.

Conflicts about church and church doctrine have divided God's people for two millennia. Many have claimed that they found the secret to church life, but their conclusions only divided us into ever-more factions. If you are waiting for an end-time manifestation of a final mechanism, organization, or leader that will accomplish what so many previous ones have failed to do, you can give up now. His church grows out of relationships, not systems. Wouldn't it be better to recognize that his church is already rising and that God is building a family that will transcend all our human attempts to define it or maintain it? Instead of trying to make it part of our group, what if we all determined to be part of his and not assume we have that all figured out? Instead of continually tweaking our programs, we can fix our attention on knowing him and loving others.

There's no need to start a revolution here and rail against the religious institutions of our day, decrying anyone who disagrees with us as legalists. I hope my words in this book have invited you into a quieter space, where you can see that the problem isn't our institutions or those who run them, but simply because we're not living as inhabitants of a new creation. We don't need to fight against what doesn't reflect him, but find a way to walk with others that does. Once we see the church as the fruit of his working rather than the fruit of ours, we can be more focused on getting to know him and letting his church unfold in loving people around us. Though we may for the moment be scattered among a vast diversity of groups that barely acknowledge one another, the time will come when those distinctions will be far less important than the camaraderie of our growing life in him.

This book is an invitation to stop looking for a group to join and to turn our hearts back to the source from which it springs. As far as the church is concerned, we're more preoccupied with the end product instead of the process that allows the church to take shape. Perhaps that's what Jesus was pointing to when he said that the kingdom always grows with the simplest of things, even the generous gift of a cup of cold water. He compared it to a mustard seed, which if planted and cared for will grow into a large bush.

The smallest choices we make have profound consequences. When you live selfishly, lie, betray trust, or take advantage of someone the world becomes a bit darker and more twisted. But every time you let his love flow through you, the world brightens. When you care about someone, forgive their failures, serve their needs, or just bring a smile to someone's face, the kingdom of God grows in the earth. If we follow him in the little things, he will take care of the big things.

If we look at the church as a river flowing through the brokenness of this age, most people want to jump in the middle rather than give attention to the headwaters from which it flows. The river actually begins where the first raindrops hit the ground and begin to connect with others. As they continue to flow down the hill other drops and collections of drops find each other. Soon rivulets form, then creeks, and finally streams that flow into rivers. That's the best way to become part of the river—not by falling into it with no connection to others around you. Everything in this kingdom works better face-to-face in caring relationships, and less well in systems intended to mass produce it.

If you want to find his church turn your heart to where the journey begins, not where it ends. It may seem counterintuitive for a book about church to recommend people give primary attention to their own individual journey, but without that journey they will not become part of that church. When people are on a journey of growing trust in Father's affection, everything about his church works well. People connect, share generously, and actually become a collaborative people that allow the church to take expression. So instead of trying to form movements and spend our time on institutional reform, we would be better off drawing near to him and helping others who want to do so also. Those are the headwaters out of which his church takes expression.

A few years ago I was invited to share with a home fellowship near us that we had been a part of for a season. This was as awkward a group as I'd ever been in and even during meals the conversation was forced and stilted. When they did talk the conversation was always about "church," what it should be, and what they could do to make it work better. In our few months with them there wasn't even a hint of conversation about their walk with Jesus and what he was doing in them.

I had no idea what I was going to share that night until a woman interrupted just before I was to begin. She wanted to share about a dream she had the previous night. Her dream consisted of two scenes—a beautiful bride standing in her wedding gown before a mirror and a groom waiting at the altar. She said it seemed to go on for hours, the bride primping and fussing with her dress, her hair, and her make-up, never able to get everything just the way she wanted. Meanwhile the groom stood alone at the altar looking at his watch as if perplexed at what could possibly be delaying his bride.

After sharing her dream she looked at the group and said, "What do you think it means? I know it's not us, but I have no idea what I'm to do with it." Everyone seemed to agree with her and no one offered her any suggestions. We are masters at ignoring the obvious, so when they asked if I was ready to share, I finally was.

"Of course it is you," I said as graciously as I could, "and almost every other Christian group throughout history. We get so focused on the church functioning the way we think it should, we end up ignoring the groom who is waiting for us to come to him." I realize our weddings today are all about the bride's special day, but in his kingdom the focus of the bride is the groom. It is his joy to make his bride ready. Our task is to be with him and let him accomplish his work instead of trying to do it for him. The more focused we are on the church, the less we'll see of her reality.

When we set our eyes on him, we will discover that we are part of a growing network of relationships filling the earth with the Lord's glory by the way they treat one another, care for people in need, share him with the world, and encourage each other in the process of transformation. You'll notice I've not made a distinction in this book between the worldwide, invisible church and the local congregation, because it is a false dichotomy. His church is not invisible. It takes shape in thousands of ways every day wherever people are living in him and finding ways to love and cooperate with one another. That can happen in traditional congregations and a thousand other ways.

His church is coming together in ways that transcend our capabilities. It won't be at a specific location, under any particular organization, or behind some charismatic leader. It will be *in* him. As you learn to live there, you will find yourself in proximity to others on a similar journey. Cooperate with his working by engaging the relationships he invites you into and watch what he can do.

Wherever you find an act of self-sacrificing love, a group of people who care for one another with generosity and compassion, you'll find his church.

Whenever you engage a conversation that illuminates the work of Jesus in your life, you'll find his church.

However you can relax into the reality of his working, rather than trying to accomplish his work on your own, you'll find his church.

How do you find his church? By drawing to him and seeing where love leads you. Every morning I ask him, "Who are you asking me to love today?" Then I live with heart and eyes wide open to the people I cross paths with and those he places on my heart to contact.

Follow him there and in the end you won't have to find the church. He'll make sure she finds you.

To Continue This Conversation You Can Join Others at *FindingChurch.com.*

Wayne's Other Titles

He Loves Me: Learning to Live in the Father's Affection
So You Don't Want to Go to Church Anymore (with Dave Coleman)
In Season: Embracing the Father's Process of Fruitfulness
A Man Like No Other (with Brad Cummings)
The Shack (in collaboration with Wm. Paul Young and Brad Cummings)
Authentic Relationships (with Clay Jacobsen)
The Naked Church

If You Want Help Exploring Your Own Relationship with Jesus

Wayne has designed free resources at Lifestream.org to help you with your journey including:

- **Transitions:** An eight-hour audio series to help you find an affection-based relationship with God.

- **Engage:** A series of six- to eight-minute videos to help you recognize how God is already building a relationship with you.

- **The Jesus Lens:** A nine-hour video series to help you read the Scriptures through the revelation of Jesus.

For more information on Wayne's travel, other books, audio collections, and DVD series you can find him at *Lifestream.org* and his podcast at *TheGodJourney.com*

Lifestream
1560 Newbury Road, Ste 1 #313 • Newbury Park, CA 91320
(805) 498-7774 • office@lifestream.org

Acknowledgments

As I said in the first chapter, I did not come upon the truths in this book alone. At every stage of my journey, I've been surrounded by people who share my passion to discover how the life of Jesus takes shape among us. We've talked long and hard, explored and questioned a thousand possibilities, and found ourselves engaging a depth of fellowship that has endeared us as lifelong friends. Some of these people live near me while others are scattered all over the world. I regret that they are too numerous to name, and if I tried it would be far too easy to leave someone out. But they know who they are and I am grateful for all the pieces they've added to seeing Jesus' church take shape in my life and in the larger world. Many of those people read this manuscript while it was still in production and offered suggestions and encouragements to help me carry on.

I do want to mention a few people whose help went over and beyond the call of duty:

Of course, no one has shared the joys and costs of traveling this road more than Sara, my wife of thirty-nine years. She is my companion, collaborator, friend, and partner through all the twists and turns and places God has led us. I will always be grateful for the joy we share together and the wisdom she has added to my life. I read every word of this book to her while it was still taking shape.

The conversations I had with Brad Cummings on a podcast called The God Journey helped solidify so many of the thoughts contained in this book. Also, the comments and letters of listeners took us down roads we might have missed. To all of them, I am grateful.

Eileen Mason of the Israel Tour Company, who was the editor of my first book many years ago, gave me some incredible insight to rework the format of this book just when I thought I had completed it. You'll never know how much more accessible to you she made the material in this book, nor how much more true to my own story.

Three dear friends helped me in the production of this final work. Kate Lapin brought her expert copyediting skills to bear on this manuscript. I'm always appreciative of her work on my projects. She makes me a better writer. Dave Aldrich of Aldrich Design put up with my wild hopes in finding just the right cover, and Nan Bishop for all the inside layout.

Finally, I want to acknowledge the board of Lifestream Ministries, dear friends without whose support and wisdom it would be very difficult for me to continue to explore some of the roads less traveled. I appreciate the friendship, humor, and insight that have allowed me to follow my heart instead of having to meet their demands.

If You'd Like to Share *Finding Church*

It is our hope that this book becomes part of a larger conversation about the nature of the church Jesus is building in our world and encourage Christ-followers to greater connection. Because it is not being handled by a book distributor it won't be found in many bookstores and thus we want to help you find a way to pass it along.

- If you would like to share this book with others, please quote from it and recommend it in your various social media outlets or post a review at Amazon.com.

- If you'd like to give print copies away to others, you will find special quantity pricing at Lifestream.org to help make that affordable.

- If you would like to retail this book on your website or at your place of business, please contact our office about wholesale pricing.

- If you'd like to provide a translation to extend it into other language groups, please contact our office for permission.